W9-BUR-447

First Lady of Detroit

THE STORY OF MARIE-THÉRÈSE GUYON, MME CADILLAC

KAREN ELIZABETH BUSH

WAYNE STATE UNIVERSITY PRESS • DETROIT

Great Lakes Books
Detroit Biography Series for Young Readers

First Lady of Detroit:
The Story of Marie-Thérèse Guyon, Mme Cadillac,
by Karen Elizabeth Bush, 2001

The Reuther Brothers—Walter, Roy, and Victor,
by Mike Smith and Pam Smith, 2001

Albert Kahn: Builder of Detroit,
by Roger Matuz, 2001

Willie Horton: Detroit's Own "Willie the Wonder,"
by Grant Eldridge and Karen Elizabeth Bush, 2001

Designed by Mary Primeau

Library of Congress Cataloging-in-Publication Data

Bush, Karen Elizabeth.
  First Lady of Detroit : the story of Marie-Thérèse Guyon, Mme.
Cadillac / Karen Elizabeth Bush.
    p. cm.— (Detroit biography series for young readers)
  Includes bibliographical references.
  ISBN 0-8143-2983-7 (cloth : alk. paper) ISBN 0-8143 2984-5 (pbk. : alk. paper)
  1. Cadillac, Marie-Thérèse Guyon—Juvenile litrature. 2. Governors' spouses—
Michigan—Detroit—Biography—Juvenile literature. 3. Cadillac, Antoine
Laumet de Lamothe, 1658–1730—Juvenile literature. 4. Detroit (Mich.)—
Biography—Juvenile literature . 5. Detroit (Mich.)—History—Juvenile litera-
ture. 6. Women pioneers—New France—Biography—Juvenile literature. 7.
Frontier and pioneer life—New France—Juvenile literature. 8. Canada—
History—To 1763 (New France)—Juvenile literature. [1. Cadillac, Marie-Thérèse
Guyon. 2. Cadillac, Antoine Laumet de Lamothe, 1658–1730. 3. Pioneers. 4.
Detroit (Mich.)—Biography. 5. Detroit (Mich.)—History. 6. Frontier and pioneer
life—New France. 7. Canada—History—To 1763 (New France)] I. Title. II. Series.
  F574.D453 C354 2001
  977.4'3401'092—dc21
                            2001001687

Fondly dedicated to

Harriet J. Berg

Detroit's modern-day Mme Cadillac
who has used dance, music, and the arts
to bring her alter ego to life
for audiences of all ages.

Contents

PREFACE

On a chilly March afternoon in the year 2000, I sat in a modern city flat and listened while Marie-Thérèse Guyon, Mme Cadillac, told me the story of her life. The fact that the woman whom I was interviewing had been dead for approximately 250 years was merely a minor inconvenience, thanks to a remarkable Detroit lady named Harriet Berg. For more than a generation—a period of time long enough for her contemporaries to finish work, retire, and make their way through a dozen post-retirement entertainments—Harriet has devoted herself to the investigation and artistic interpretation of the life of the first woman to arrive at Fort Pontchartrain, Ville du Détroit. It has been suggested—with tongue not too far in cheek—that, without Harriet, there wouldn't even *be* any Madame Cadillac. Certainly her research and research that she has inspired not only have promoted Antoine Laumet de Lamothe Cadillac's wife from a postscript on the pages of history to a living, viable contributor to that history, but also have added substantially to our knowledge of the historical events in which Marie-Thérèse played a part. On that March afternoon, in bold, sweeping strokes, Harriet Berg outlined the events that made up the life of her alter ego—and this little book was born.

When my own research delved into the earlier years of Marie-Thérèse's life, I was amazed to find I could discover much about a youth thought to be undocumented simply by piecing together the things already known about the places and times that Marie-Thérèse lived. Thus, while a necessary percentage of this biographical novel is fictionalized, almost every word or episode has some grounding in fact. Surprisingly it is those events which were most bizarre that were easiest to document. Nor was Marie-Thérèse an exception to the world in which she lived. One has only to read the astounding tale of Madeleine de Verchères (chapter 14) to realize that not only was Marie-Thérèse Guyon not an ordinary woman, she most certainly did not live in ordinary times.

For the benefit of educators, historians, and young readers who wish "to know more about it," a compendium of historical notes is included in an appendix to the actual book. These pages sort out fact from fiction, and, when taken with the bibliography listing sources for most of the story, are intended to be an historical guide and a useful teaching tool.

First Lady of Detroit is intended for young adult audiences—appealing to readers ranging from age ten to age eighteen but with a specific focus on twelve- to fifteen-year-olds. I hope that the research that has gone into the book and the remarkable presence of Marie-Thérèse herself will render it entertaining and useful to readers of all ages.

Finally, I cannot conclude this foreword without acknowledging the immense assistance provided me by the nuns living today in the same Ursuline Monastery in Québec City that housed and schooled Marie-Thérèse and her friends. In particular I am grateful for the support and sense of humor of Marie Marchand, o.s.u., historian and librarian, and her colleague Sister Louise, whose English proved sufficient to overcome my extremely limited acquaintance with French!

> Karen Elizabeth Bush
> Rochester, Michigan
> June 11, 2000

❖ 1 ❖

A Tale of New France

The sunlight was so bright the children felt as if they could touch it. The stones in the courtyard caught each ray and reflected it back, making the warm air seem warmer yet. The year was 1745, and all the old people were saying that France hadn't seen an autumn this hot and dry since the last century. The farmers talked about drought and worried about the crops. Adults were sure that the dry fall weather meant that the winter would bring cold and rain and disease. People laid in stores and said there would be a famine if the next spring was too wet for planting. But the children didn't care. They cared only that today it was warm, the sun shone, and lessons were finished until tomorrow. And the best thing about this kind of weather was that, on nice days, Madame Cadillac came out to take the sun.

Madame Cadillac was a very old lady—older than anyone else in the village. She once had many children of her own—born so long ago that some of them already had grown old and died. Now it was as though the young people of Castelsarrasin were her children. In a very special way, she belonged to them and they to her. Because she was old, Madame Cadillac lived with the Carmelite sisters, but the children knew that once she had been very grand. She had been wife to the governor and once lived in the governor's palace. Before that, she had been welcome at the glorious court of France's great Sun King, Louis XIV. And before that . . . before that. . . . Before that, Marie Thérèse Guyon Cadillac had known such adventures that the children scarcely could believe them, much less imagine them.

Boys and girls jostled for position at the far end of the courtyard. If one looked very carefully, a small, white head could just be seen in their midst, almost hidden by the brightly colored clothing of some of the taller children. Madame Cadillac sat in her special chair and held court in the sunshine, her gaily clad admirers gathered at her feet. "Tell us more stories, Madame, please?" a girl cried. "Yes, tell us!" A small dark-haired boy pushed into the center of the group. "Tell us about *Nouvelle France*—about New France. Tell us about Québec."

The old lady smiled at him. "You've heard it all before, René. Don't you want to hear something different?"

"No!" "No!" There was a chorus of shouts. "No, tell us about New France, please?"

"Please tell us about the time you lived in the New World, Madame." The little girl who'd spoken first came forward to sit next to René. "You make the stories seem new every time."

"Well, there you are, *chérie!* The stories seem new to me, too. Every time I think about New France, and my children, and Antoine, it's as if I am living it all over again." Marie-Thérèse smiled and tipped her head back, thinking about where to begin. Perhaps almost at the beginning. Perhaps there would be time to tell the whole story before winter came to take the sun away. She took a breath and began to speak.

⚜ ⚜ ⚜

"Come on, tell us again, Al. Please?" The girl who had spoken propped herself up on one elbow and stared pleadingly at her friend.

The late October sun beat down on three heads, one dark, one fair, and one satiny black. The enormous ash tree at the back of the monastery grounds was the girls' favorite place to meet. Today they were using its roots as a sort of pillow, leaning back against the dry bark as they watched the clouds pass by overhead.

"Oh, Marie-Thérèse! You've heard it all so many times! You've memorized it by now." The girl called Al was half-amused, half-exasperated.

The three were dressed almost identically in sober blue gowns with fresh white kerchiefs at their necks. Each had an equally white mobcap that was supposed to be on her head. But today mobcap strings were hot and sticky under the chin, and the moment the girls were away from Mother Mary's watchful eye the caps had come off. Swung by those same strings, a mobcap made a handy bag in which to carry a bit of bread kept over from the midday dinner, or maybe a bright bird feather to be saved for the little ones in the convent school. Marie-Thérèse, still waiting for Al's answer, was a little taller and perhaps a little older than the others. Her eyes danced gaily, her cheeks were red, and her whole bearing spoke of energy. Her dark brown hair was tied back in an attempt to keep it orderly, but like Marie-Thérèse herself, it seemed ready to burst forth at any moment. Her friend Al was dark, dark. Her slender brown face was framed by hair that lay in braids as smooth and black as a crow's feathers. Al lay perfectly still, but it was easy to imagine her in motion—maybe running, or swimming—doing something that would whisk her away to disappear in the forest darkness beyond the convent walls. The third girl, Anne, was fair-haired and sturdy, a little heavier than the other two. She was quieter than the others, but she'd proven over and over that she was the best sort of friend to have when there was any kind of trouble.

Marie-Thérèse Guyon, Anne Picoté de Belestre, and Denise Al-soom-se all were students at the convent school of the Ursuline monastery in Québec—the trading center of New France. They had been best friends as long as any of them could remember. First they had shared the loneliness of being sent away to school, and then they learned that they also could share their love of discovery and adventure. In fact, poor Mother Mary of the Angels often felt that she spent more time on her knees praying over these three and their "adventures" than for all the other children in her charge!

But 1686 was a time for adventure—the best of times. French exploration of the New World was at its most exciting—both for the French explorers and traders and for the Algonquin and Abenaki people who lived in the newly discovered lands. The Algonquin tribes had long fought with the Iroquois to the south. Now the French were there to stand with the Algonquin. There was heavy competition with the English, who were settling the lands to the south, but trade flourished. Ships crossed the ocean to France carrying rich furs that had been trapped in the wilderness. The same ships returned bringing wonderful things that could not yet be found in Québec. Because the new country had made their families wealthy, Marie-Thérèse and Anne went to school just as if they had been the daughters of famous dukes or counts or even royalty. Because the French were his trading partners, Denise Al-soom-se's father, a chief of the Abenaki, was able to have his daughter schooled as a French lady. Going to school was all part of the adventure. If the girls learned to be fine ladies, they would make fine marriages. If they married rich traders, the settlement in Québec would grow and trade would grow even more.

But wealth and trade and future marriage were far from Marie-Thérèse's mind today. "Well?" she demanded, looking again at Al-soom-se.

"Yes, tell us again," Anne spoke up. "You make it sound almost like a song."

Outnumbered, Al-soom-se sighed. "Oh, all right." She sat up and crossed her legs in the way Anne called "tailor-fashion." Her voice changed a little, and now when she began to speak, though the sun still shone brightly, the air around her seemed to quiver. Marie-Thérèse and Anne held their breaths.

"It all must begin with my brother's story." Al-soom-se had closed her eyes and was rocking slightly from side to side. "He was young and very, very brave. He knew of the great waters in the lands where the sun sets, and he wanted to see them for himself. He went to the council house. He begged the wise leaders to let him go to the lands of the Huron and bring back stones from the edge of the great waters. 'You may go, young brother,' the elders said. 'But before you return, remember that you must also bring back something of value to all the Abenaki—not just something for yourself.' And they asked the Great Spirit to speed him on his journey.

"The winter had just left us when he set out. The Great Spirit brought him many rabbits to eat. He walked by moving waters, and the waters were full of fish to catch. He followed the sun, and each day the sun stayed before him a little longer, leading him further and further toward the land of the Huron.

"One night as he slept, he was awakened by sounds that were not made by the creatures of the forest. He heard laughter and loud voices. He listened carefully. He understood enough of the words to know that he was sharing the forest with an Iroquois war party. Now the Iroquois are the enemy of the Abenaki. They take forest lands that have been given to people of the Abenaki by the Great Spirit. They pursue the Huron, and they have driven the Ojibwe and the Potawatomi into lands that lie beyond the great waters. If they had known my brother was there, they would have killed him.

"My brother crept away into the forest. Now, each day as he traveled toward the sun, he must be careful. He must not travel so fast that he overtook the Iroquois, or so slowly that other Iroquois using the same trail could overtake him. No more could he build a fire to cook the fish he caught. No more could he leave snares to catch rabbits, because a snare took time and would show the Iroquois he was nearby. He had only the dried corn he carried to eat. But he was careful, and he kept going. He was determined to see the great waters for himself.

"Then one day the moving water that he followed ceased to move and opened out into a great lake—the first of the great waters. He stood there on the shore and looked at water as far as

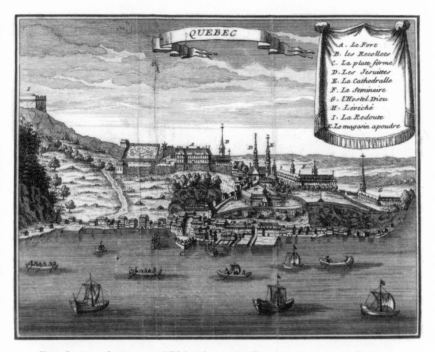

THE CITY OF QUÉBEC IN 1701. This is Québec (Upper Town and Lower Town) as it looked when Marie-Thérèse lived there. Building F., "Le Seminaire" is the Ursuline monastery. It's right between the cathedral and the Hôtel Dieu. (I. B. Scotin, *Québec, Québec,* National Archives of Canada, C-004696.)

15

THE ORIGINAL PEOPLE OF *NOUVELLE FRANCE*. All around the city of Québec, the forests were home for several tribes of woodland people. This is probably a temporary campsite. Families are sheltering in tepees covered with birch bark. The large canoe also is made of birch bark. You can tell that the men in this picture have been trading with the settlers, because several of them have on European clothing. (William Armstrong, *Indian Encampment*, National Archives of Canada, C-040293.)

16

the eye could see, and that night the sun sank into the water ahead of him. The Great Spirit must have been pleased that my brother had come so far, for he gave him a reward. There in the reeds by the shore lay a canoe, waiting for him—waiting to help him cross the waters. It was damaged. Perhaps the Iroquois had left it behind. My brother mended the canoe and used it to go on, paddling through the calm waters along the shore. After many days he came to a place where a broad stream of water flowed into the lake. He knew this came from the next great water, and so he turned and followed the moving water upstream. For a while he could paddle along easily, but then the water moved faster and faster toward him and turned white with its speed. He had to return to shore. He did not carry the canoe with him toward the sun, but hid it well and once again began to walk. Now his path followed the sun during the day as well as in the evening, and he knew he had turned toward the land of the Iroquois.

"The sound of the moving water made it hard to hear even the birds in the trees, and when he woke the next morning, he discovered that he had camped very near the Iroquois party—no more than the distance that a small child can run. This time, the Great Spirit chose to test my brother's speed, for the Iroquois saw him and heard him. When a warrior has a duty—to bring home something of value to the Abenaki—he is not a coward if he runs away from twelve men who want to kill him. And my brother ran. He ran and he ran, and all the time that he ran, the noise of the water was loud in his ears.

"Suddenly he came to a place where he could see all the water in the world tumbling down toward him. All he could think was that the Great Spirit had led him to where he could see this, and safety must lie in the place where the water fell. Behind him, the Iroquois stopped and pointed at him, laughing. As he ran closer and closer to the edge of the falling water, they were sure that he would be drowned. The rocks over which he climbed and ran were wet and slippery. Winds blew in many directions. He could hardly breathe because the water that fell down before him seemed to fill the air. Then, suddenly, he saw behind the water a place where the rocks made a sort of cave. He jumped and slipped, and the Great Spirit helped him hold on to the rocks. The water fell all around him, but he was almost dry. The noise was so great it made a kind of silence.

17

MARIE DE L'INCARNATION. Before Marie-Thérèse Guyon was born, an Ursuline nun named Marie de l'Incarnation came to Québec and established a school where both *canadienne* and *amérindienne* (native) girls could study. Because of this, Marie-Thérèse was able to have the sort of education that, in France, she could have received only if her father was a nobleman. This sketch is a "post-mortem" portrait, meant to pay tribute to Marie de l'Incarnation after her death. For that reason, the artist has drawn her with her eyes shut. (Frontispiece, *Les Ursulines de Québec*. Québec: C. Darveau, 1863. Reprinted courtesy Archives of the Ursulines of Québec.)

"When night came, my brother made his way back to the rocks on the shore. The Iroquois were gone. He could see where they had packed up their camp and moved on toward the sun. He thought a moment, and then turned back toward the lands of the Abenaki. He had seen the first of the great waters and the Great Spirit had saved him from the Iroquois. He was content.

"The trail homeward was an easy one. When he came again to the council of the elders, they asked him what he had brought that was of value to the Abenaki. He told them this story. It will be told around the campfires of the Abenaki until the end of time."

Al-soom-se was silent. In the distance, a bird sang. It sounded oddly out of place. Then a bell rang. "Bong!" It rang again.

"Oh dear!" Marie-Thérèse scrambled to her feet, followed by the other girls. "That's for vespers, and here comes Mother Mary."

A blue and gray shape came striding toward them from the direction of the chapel. "Girls! Girls!" Mother Mary's voice could be heard clearly, even over the full length of the convent grounds.

"We're in for it now," hissed Anne. "We were late for mass this morning, and the only way we got out of washhouse duty was to absolutely promise we'd be at vespers!" And the three broke into a most unladylike run.

✣ 2 ✣
The Price of Adventure

Marie-Thérèse straightened up slowly. For hours, she had been lifting sodden clothing in and out of wash water. Her back hurt so much that she moved like an old woman. "I feel as old as Mother Athanasius!" she said out loud.

"Me, too," groaned Anne. "How can just twenty-three nuns have this much laundry?"

"There are twenty-eight of us, if you count me and the rest of the lay sisters, and we work and get dirty and need clean clothes too, whether or not we've taken orders. And so do all your fellow students who are full boarders. This lot happens to be their linen." Young Sister Cécile plumped down an enormous heap of soiled bed linen as she spoke. She stepped back and grinned at her three exhausted charges. "Just be glad you aren't doing the laundry for the Jesuit hospital! Anyway, this is the last. When these are boiled clean and spread to dry, you'll be done for the day. Shall I tell Mother Mary that you are truly penitent as well as being truly tired? It would be a shame if you had to spend any more time in here with me. You need every spare minute to get ready for the pageant."

The girls looked at each other. They'd almost forgotten about the pageant. In less than a week, it would be the Feast of Ste. Ursula. Many important people from the city and from the Jesuit college next door would come to share in the festivities. There would be many special events in honor of the saint, and the students were to put on a pageant. All the monastery pupils would take part, whether they were full boarders who lived entirely at the monastery, half-boarders who took their noon meal with the regular boarders but slept at home, or just day students. Each pupil had a part.

The idea for the pageant was simple enough. Since they were taught by the sisters of the Ursuline Monastery of Québec, the students planned to act out the story of the monastery's 1639 founding. The trouble was that Mother Superior and two other sisters actually had been there when it all began. Even though the monastery had been founded forty-seven years ago—a longer time than many people lived—the sisters remembered it as if it had happened in the last week. The pageant would have to be perfect. Marie-Thérèse sighed. "I don't suppose they'll still want me to play the part of Mother Marie de l'Incarnation anyway," she shrugged. "Not any more. Not after this. I don't think people who found monasteries are the kind of people who get in trouble for not going to services."

"Don't you be so sure. You may not be our most saintly student, but you still are the tallest and the oldest," chuckled Sister Cécile. "How do you three get into so much trouble, anyway? It's not as though you don't know the rules. You've attended the school since 1683—and you're great girls now, fourteen or fifteen years old. Your friends are married by now. Some of them have babies of their own, and yet we can't even count on you to set a good example for the primary students—for *les petites!*" Sister Cécile continued to smile, but she shook her head a little at the same time. She used a stick to stir the laundry in the pot before her. "We need more water from the well. Do I have a volunteer?"

"I'll get it." Al-soom-se was out the door even as she spoke. She always felt a little trapped in the big masonry buildings. It was good to go out in the clear fall air, even if it meant carrying heavy buckets of water. She pushed the well cover to one side and drew up the clear, cold water with a small bucket. She used the bucket to fill two larger wooden pails. Then she fastened the heavy pails to the ends of a wooden yoke. With the yoke across her shoulders, she steadied both pails with her hands and made her way back into the washhouse.

"Thank you, Denise." Sister Cécile smiled as Al-soom-se turned sideways to get through the door.

"See? That's part of it. We get in trouble for that, too." Marie-Thérèse apparently was answering Sister Cécile's earlier question. "Mother Mary doesn't like it when we call Al by her Abenaki name.

We use her Christian name, too, during lessons, but Mother Mary doesn't want us to call her 'Al-soom-se' at all."

"She doesn't like the fact that 'Al-soom-se' means 'Independent Woman,'" added Anne. "She says we are too independent as it is."

"I think it's more because she keeps comparing me to Agnes Wesk-wes," said Al, setting down the heavy buckets. "Which pot needs the water? You know Agnes was here with us in 1683. When she graduated and went home to her parents, she got so homesick for the sisters, she begged to come back. And then, when she did come back, the first thing she did was get sick and die. It makes her like some kind of a saint. I mean, she really was a wonderful person, but she just was different from the rest of us. She really wanted to be a nun."

"Well, you came back, too," said Sister Cécile reasonably.

"That was just for the same reason Marie-Thérèse and I did," laughed Anne. "We're all too old to be home and not be married!" She ducked just in time to avoid the armload of dirty laundry that Marie-Thérèse threw at her.

As tired as they were, the three managed to spread the last linen sheet out to dry while the sun was still high in the sky. "Now what?" asked Anne.

"I know what I want to do, but there's not enough time today," answered Marie-Thérèse. "Anyway, it'd just get us in more trouble."

"What?" chorused Anne and Al-soom-se.

"I want to go into town. Not the Upper Town where the governor's palace and the Jesuit community is, but down the staircase into the Lower Town—right down to the water. It has been a busy year for the fur traders—so busy that they have run out of goods to trade for furs." Anne and Al-soom-se nodded. They knew that. "I just heard that the *coureurs de bois,* the 'runners of the woods,' are getting ready to make one last trip to resupply the traders. Right this minute, they're probably gathering up supplies to take with them into the wilderness. I know the *coureurs de bois* can be wild and crazy, but I love it when they are in town. 'Woods runners' is so perfect a name for what they do and the life they lead. They explore. They go places in their canoes that we'll never see. We can't go along, but we could go watch them as they get ready to leave."

21

"You really don't plan to be in that pageant, do you? You're just looking for trouble," teased Al-soom-se.

"Maybe we wouldn't get caught. If we wait until after lessons tomorrow, we could go out when the day students leave to go home. I don't really want to spend any time in town. I just want to see and . . . and *feel* what it's like. And then we'd come right back here. It's warm. There will be windows open everyplace. It's getting dark early now. I know we could climb back into the student dormitory without anyone seeing us."

"And if they look for us while we're gone?" asked Anne.

"We'll just tell them that we went into the woods to practice for the pageant. Mother Mary will scold, but she'll be pleased that we're taking the pageant seriously. Besides, it's true, Anne. If you are going to dress like a *coureur de bois* for the pageant, you need to know what they look and act like."

"That's an awful lot of climbing and hiking to just turn right around and come back again," sighed Anne. "But," and she smiled, "it's probably as close as any of us except Al-soom-se will get to the wilderness. I'm game!"

"I've got an idea." Al-soom-se had been sitting on the ground, knees pulled up to her chin, but now she jumped to her feet. "Why don't we wear the *coureur de bois* costumes from the pageant? If we just wear the shirts and trousers and leave off the scarves and things, we'll look like some of the boys in town. We can pull the caps down over our hair. We'll be able to move faster than we can in skirts. We maybe can go and get back in time to stay out of trouble."

"And as we leave, we'll look as if we are brothers of some of the day students—come to walk them home. It's a grand idea!" laughed Marie-Thérèse.

Québec, where the Monastery of the Ursulines was located, was really two small towns: Upper Town and Lower Town. In Upper Town, officials lived and worked at the Château St. Louis—an elegant and impressive building that sat atop the cliffs overlooking the St. Lawrence River. From its upper windows, you could see forests, water, or hills, all depending on which way you turned. Not far from the château, the Jesuit priests had built their college and hospital.

COUREURS DE BOIS. *Coureurs de bois* were explorers and adventurers as well as being hunters and traders. Their name means "woods runners." Often they came from wealthy families, but they chose the adventure and excitement of living in the wilderness. These two are dressed in buckskin (tanned deer hides) though some *coureurs* preferred brightly colored woolen clothing. Those fringes weren't just for decoration. The long pieces of hide could be torn off and used just like pieces of string. By the time a buckskin shirt was old and worn out, most of its fringe would be gone—used up to mend and sew things. (*Left:* C. W. Jefferys, *Coureur de Bois,* National Archives of Canada, C-069731. *Right:* Arthur Heming, *Coureur de Bois,* National Archives of Canada, C-005746.)

These, too, were enormous stone buildings—larger than many in Paris. The Ursuline Monastery was on one side of the Jesuit college. The monastery buildings were older and smaller than the huge Jesuit structures, but they still looked important because there were so many of them clustered together. The largest of them had a cupola topped with a tall cross. The cupola could be seen for some distance down the river.

On the other side of the college and the great church of Notre Dame stood the Hôtel Dieu—the Jesuit hospital. Then there was a public square. Along the square, there were a few government buildings. The governor lived in the Château St. Louis and didn't need his own palace, so that was about all there was to Upper Town.

A huge staircase had been built against the cliff, making it possible to walk easily from Upper Town to Lower Town. Lower Town was full of low buildings—mostly made of wood, though according to law all of them had to have masonry gables. Each one had a roof of cedar shingles. In this year of 1686, just about every building was new. Four years earlier, the entire Lower Town had caught fire and burned to the ground. Now, rebuilt just as it had been before, it looked solid and safe, but fire remained a threat.

Freed from skirts that wrapped around ankles and feet, Marie-Thérèse, Anne, and Al-soom-se ran and trotted and ran again along the full length of the cliff. Breathless, they hurled themselves at the steps. "This is going to be much easier going in this direction," said Al-soom-se, looking over her head at the cliff rising high above. "I'm not looking forward to climbing back up there!"

"Can we stop a minute?" gasped Anne. "That was a long way to run."

Halfway down the long staircase, the girls paused and looked down. Lower Town was spread out below them, gleaming in the late afternoon sun.

"Did the governor ever get his fire buckets?" wondered Marie-Thérèse. Just the last year, Governor Denonville had written to King Louis XIV, explaining that the town had no money to spare. He begged for two hundred crowns worth of fire buckets.

"I think so," replied Anne. "My mother complained last fall that she wasn't able to get fine fabrics at the milliner's shop. The shopkeeper told her that his latest shipment of goods hadn't even been loaded on board because the ship's hold was full of an emergency supply of leather buckets. I guess they were sent on that particular ship because it was leaving just about the time the King received the governor's letter."

"You can see why the town burned so easily," remarked Al-soom-se. Not only were the houses wooden, this time of year most of them had great mounds of firewood piled next to them. Some buildings were almost hidden by stacks of hay. The hay was necessary because there were so many cows in Lower Town. "It would be better if there were some way to get water from the river into the town—I mean to put out a fire," Al-soom-se went on. "Buckets don't hold much water."

"I understand there are people who want to get an iron pump from France. A few men working a pump can move a lot of water in a hurry. But for some reason the governor isn't letting them order one. My uncle François was talking about it the last time I visited him." Marie-Thérèse had started down the steps again. "Let's hurry! We don't want to get there just as everything stops for the day."

The girls worked their way down the streets toward the waterfront. The town was very clean, and not just because it was newly built. There were laws written to keep it that way. The housefronts looked clean and were clean. One law said that each man who owned a house had to dig a gutter in the middle of his street. The open gutters were smelly, but because they were in the middle of the street, they were as far away from the houses as they possibly could be. Another law ordered that all garbage had to be carried down to the river and thrown into it. This kept trash from piling up in the gutters, and the gutters drained freely into the St. Lawrence. Yet another law made people responsible for their dogs, and ordered that all dogs be brought indoors before nine o'clock at night.

"There you are, Marie-Thérèse," cried Al-soom-se. "See? See the canoes?" At last they had reached the level of the docks. Large ships were anchored in the river, but nearer shore they could see where enormous birch-bark canoes had been tied to the pier. They looked like small, mastless ships—each one nearly thirty-five feet long and as wide as a man is tall. Each canoe could hold fourteen men and well over a ton of trade goods or furs. Today they held more bundles than people. Those that had fewer than half a dozen *coureurs* aboard had room for as much as two tons of food and trade goods, and even muskets and ammunition. One or two of the canoes already were loaded and, with a man or so to guard them, they waited patiently for the hurried voyage to begin. Others still rode high in the water, bobbing up and down excitedly with the motion of the river. Merchants and other men moved to and fro. Working closest to the canoes, the girls could see figures dressed in heavy woolen shirts and colorful sashes. One or two wore buckskin—soft leather made from deerskin and fringed and decorated like Abenaki clothing.

The girls stood there and watched as long as they dared. There wasn't that much to see, really—just men loading and carrying things and shouting happily to each other. But you could feel the excitement in the air. Some of the shouted words came across the docks to the watching girls. For the most part, the *coureurs de bois* were boasting, bragging of the success of their travels and talking of adventures to come. One man looked up and saw the three "boys" watching him. "Here, you lads!" he called. "Come over here! Give us a hand with this!"

"We'd better leave—NOW," hissed Anne. No one argued. Backing up rapidly, the girls worked their way into the sheltering streets of the town. Out of sight of the docks, they turned and ran.

"We needed to head back anyway," Marie-Thérèse panted. "It'll be almost supper time when we get there."

But there was to be no supper that night—at least not for Marie-Thérèse, Anne, and Al-soom-se. Nor did they climb into conveniently open dormitory windows. Instead, the tired little group was halted a few yards in front of the gate to the monastery. One of the older lay sisters stood there, arms folded, watching for them. "You are to go straight to Mother Mary," the sister spoke sternly. "Now." And she turned on her heel without so much as a "hello and where have you been" and marched away from them.

It was a forlorn trio that stood before the mistress of students. For a long while, Mother Mary gazed at them in absolute silence. Finally she spoke. "I am *maîtresse de division*—the supervisor of three levels of students. I have *les petites*—little ones fresh from home in my charge. I have *les moyennes*—girls who are just beginning to feel at home here, and to know what it is to be a lady of New France. I have *les grandes*—the oldest ones, girls who are ready to leave here and marry. And I have you three. I ask the good Lord where I have failed with you three! What ever were you thinking?"

"I wanted to watch the *coureurs de bois* get ready for the last resupply trip, Sister. It was all my fault, really. It was all my idea. Please don't be angry with Anne and Al . . . Anne and Denise." Marie-Thérèse had pulled off her *coureur de bois* cap. Her hair, damp with sweat and curling around her face, looked like some kind of dark brown halo. She twisted the cap in her hands and untwisted it again as she spoke.

Mother Mary sighed. "At least you are honest, and you are fair. But I think, in this escapade, you all had a part. There is no real harm done. You are home and you are safe. But you are very, very lucky. You could have walked into great trouble. Remember, you are the responsibility of this monastery. If you had been hurt or injured in any way, the blame for it would have fallen on us here. We are your guardians. This is the problem. It is not just that you placed yourself in danger. You have not thought of the trouble you bring to others—only of your own pleasure. Go now—immediately—to chapel and pray. Pray that God will teach you that other people may be hurt by your recklessness. And after you finish your prayers, dress in your proper clothing again and return the costumes to the place that you found them. Tonight you will go to bed without supper, and tomorrow you will report again to Sister Cécile. Tell her she will have help in the wash-house for the remainder of the week."

The girls turned to leave. "And Marie-Thérèse?" Marie-Thérèse turned back to look at Mother Mary. "You particularly also should thank Sister Cécile. As further punishment, you were to have been removed from the pageant, but Sister Cécile has intervened for you. She feels that your actions are irresponsible but not wicked, and that they stem from an adventurous spirit. She has reminded us that the venerable Marie de l'Incarnation too was a woman of adventurous spirit."

"Yes, Mother. Thank you, Mother," said Marie-Thérèse. Head down, she walked toward the chapel.

⚜ 3 ⚜
Fire!

Marie-Thérèse shifted her knees slightly, seeking a more comfortable position on the hard floor. It was October 20, 1686—only one more day before the pageant. She sighed. It was hard to keep her mind on the words of the mass. She felt rather than saw Mother Mary shoot a warning glance in her direction. She wondered if the tall Jesuit priest had been told he had three penitents in his congregation. She shifted again, guiltily. She had been selfish. She knew that. She should not have left the monastery grounds. She should not have involved Anne and Al-soom-se in her prank. She should not have worried Mother Mary. Sister Cécile was right. She was far too old for such silliness. *"Mea culpa,"* she whispered to herself. "My fault. *Mea maxima culpa."*

"Shhhhhhhhhhhhhhhh!" hissed Anne, off to her right.

Before them, the priest moved swiftly before the altar. He was tall and graceful, and his vestments swooped elegantly as he knelt to place a ceremonial kiss on the white cloth covering the altar. Marie-Thérèse fancied that their embroidered length wafted the smell of the altar candle smoke down toward her. It seemed to fan the warm aroma all the way past the choir where the nuns knelt reverently and on out into the nave. There in the open part of the church, the lay sisters and students waited in worshipful silence. Marie-Thérèse sniffed the candle smoke and tried to think about holy things.

"Dominus vobiscum," the priest sang. "The Lord be with you." His voice was high and thin—like the rest of him, Marie-Thérèse chuckled to herself.

"Hush, Marie-Thérèse!" This time it was Al-soom-se who jabbed her friend sharply in the ribs. *"Et cum spiritu tuo,"* the nuns sang back obediently. "And with thy spirit."

The candle smoke smell was stronger. "That's funny," Marie-Thérèse thought. "He's not moving now."

Indeed, the priest looked almost like a statue, he was so still. *"Pretiosi corporis . . ."* he began the words of the day's thanksgiving.

Outside the church, there was a confusion of voices. Still on their knees, eyes tightly closed and thinking as much of their speeches in tomorrow's pageant as of the words of the service, Anne and Al-soom-se reached the same conclusion. That much noise had to have been made by Marie-Thérèse. From where they knelt on either side of her, they both jabbed at the same time.

"Hey!" yelped Marie-Thérèse into the hushed silence of the service.

Before the others could scold her, everyone heard the parlor bell begin to ring. It rang frantically—again and again and again. The girls had never heard of such an interruption to mass. In less than a moment of that wild clanging, it was obvious that something was terribly wrong. The priest began to pray so rapidly that it was impossible to understand him. He was almost to the blessing now. Mother Superior didn't wait for him to finish. She stood up and walked rapidly across the choir and toward the corridor leading to the church. To see Mother Marie Drouet de Jésus turn her back on the service was almost more alarming than anything else. *"Ite, Missa est*—go, the Mass is ended," the priest gabbled after her departing figure.

Before the nuns could respond with the final words of the service, Mother Superior was back in the doorway.

"It is fire," she said unnecessarily. Smoke was pouring from the corridor into the church. She raised her voice and gave the clear order, *"All is lost! The whole house is in flames. Get to a place of safety as soon as possible."*

The smallest pupils began to cry. "You, Marie-Thérèse, Anne!" called Mother Mary. "Take the little ones with you and go!" Never had the girls been so quick to obey. Blessing the discipline the children had been taught, they formed the terrified *petites* into lines and marched them out of the building. Behind Anne, Al-soom-se found a way through the thickening smoke for *les moyennes.* At the very last of the middle students came the remaining *grandes,* followed by the nuns and lay sisters.

Once she and her small charges were in the safety of the open air, Marie-Thérèse paused. She looked back at the monastery, unbelieving. This couldn't be possible! She spun toward where

THE FIRST AND SECOND MONASTERIES. The first two Ursuline monasteries in Québec were built on the same foundation, so the above picture of the burning of the first monastery probably looks a lot like the second monastery did when *it* was on fire.

This picture shows the church and dormitory of the second monastery, which was built in 1651 and burned in 1686. After the second monastery burned, a third monastery was begun. Some of its buildings stand today. ("Incendie du Premier Monastère [1650]" and "Église et Pensionnat du Second Monastère [bàti en 1651; brulé en 1686]." *Les Ursulines de Québec.* Québec: C. Darveau, 1863. Reprinted courtesy Archives of the Ursulines of Québec.)

the old kitchen stood at the far north end of the monastery. The kitchen was the first of the string of buildings leading toward the church. Or it had been. Now all Marie-Thérèse could see was a ball of flame where the kitchen was supposed to be. The great tall chimney that rose from the open hearth where cooking was done was nowhere to be seen. "The fire began in the kitchen chimney," she heard someone say.

It didn't really matter where the fire had begun. It was all too obvious where it was going. The wind blew strongly from the north. It blew the fire before it—from the kitchen to the main building, from the main building to the chapel, from the chapel to the church. In this mild fall, the trees of the forest had held their brilliantly colored leaves. The leaves were there now—beautiful, rustling and moving in the wind. But now their color moved from the forest to the inside of the monastery wall, like paint smearing past the edges of a drawing. And once inside the wall the color didn't rustle. It roared and crackled and snapped as it twisted about. As Marie-Thérèse stood and stared, wild oranges and reds began to cover up the sober gray of the monastery buildings.

"How can it burn stone?" one of *les petites* begged.

"It's the pine walls and partitions and flooring that are burning," one of the sisters replied gently. "The stone and masonry just crumbles from the heat." The sister who spoke gave the child a small shove and then ran back toward the church. A blue-gray knot of nuns wavered about the door. From where she stood, Marie-Thérèse could feel the heat of the flames on her face. She could only imagine how terrible it must feel that close to the fire.

She saw one figure, and then another, emerge from the church. The sisters stumbled and ran, carrying altar cloths and vestments—not many of either. The entire group was with Marie-Thérèse now, coughing and gasping for breath. "So little saved, so little saved," mourned Mother Athanasius. "But we have the monastery records, and we have the altar vestments."

"What about the reliquary? Which of you has the reliquary?" Mother Mary of the Angels was looking about her as though she somehow suspected that one of the students had carried it off as a joke.

The heavily decorated box containing the precious relics of Ste. Ursula was not with the vestments. It had to be still in the

31

church. The sisters looked at each other, trying to absorb the horror of this final loss. Behind them, the fire marched onward. The schoolroom was gone with its books and furnishings, and now the flames lapped at the northernmost end of the chapel. Marie-Thérèse squinted her eyes against the smoke and glare. Surely that wasn't someone running toward the church—but it was! With the skirts of her habit bunched around her hips so that she could run faster, Sister Cécile charged down the slight incline and into the doorway that led to the choir. "Holy Father, protect her!" breathed Sister Madeleine, another lay sister.

It appeared that Sister Madeleine's prayer would be in vain. No sooner had the scrap of blue habit disappeared into the smoky darkness than the flames passed the chapel and reached the church. In moments, fire broke out of the church windows.

The sisters were beyond tears. "We must pray for her soul," said Mother Superior. In response, a steady, sad murmuring rose from the little group. Marie-Thérèse's throat ached. Sister Cécile, with her wide smile and country sense of humor, was her favorite of all the monastery residents.

"But look! Look!" One of the littlest children shrieked. "Look! There she is! There's Sister Cécile! She's all right!"

"Yes, yes! There she is! But how will we ever. . . . She is still lost. . . ." Cries of joy and concern filled the air, almost as loud as the crackle of the advancing flames. Blue showed for a moment in an attic window, and then gray, and then an arm and a leg, as Sister Cécile, pushing the reliquary in front of her, scrambled out onto the roof of the church.

Now the whole monastery grounds were filled with running figures. Men, women, and children from the village, led by those who had given the first alarm, were drawing bucket after bucket of water from the wells. They passed the buckets from hand to hand in a long line that reached from the wells to the church. One of the men near the front of the bucket brigade heard the shouting and looked over his head. Above him, legs dangling over the very edge of the roof, sat Sister Cécile.

Someone brought a ladder. It reached barely a third of the way to the roof, but the man didn't hesitate. He climbed up to the top rung and stood there, pressed hard against the wall of the church. "Sister, do you think you can hang down from the roof and stand on my shoulders?" he called.

THE SECOND MONASTERY BEFORE THE FIRE. This drawing of the second monastery—the one that Marie-Thérèse watched burn in 1686—
gives us a better idea how high the roof was through which Sister
Cécile escaped. (Preface to part 2, *Glimpses of the Monastery: A Brief Sketch
of the History of the Ursulines of Quebec During Two Hundred Years, by a
Member of the Community.* Québec: C. Darveau, 1875.)

"First take the reliquary," gasped Sister Cécile. As she spoke,
she bent and clamped the reliquary between her feet. She turned
around, knelt at the edge of the roof, and gripped the edge of the
masonry with her hands. "Be quick," she said. "I can hold on for
a while, but I don't know how long."

She dropped over the side, dangling from the roof edge, the
precious box held tightly between her feet. The townsman
reached up as high as he could and took the reliquary in both
hands. Steadied by others behind him on the ladder, he backed
down just far enough to hook one arm through the ladder and
pass the reliquary to the man behind him. Then he went up the
ladder again.

Sister Cécile had found a ridge of masonry against which to
brace her feet. "Now, Sister," said her rescuer, "drop straight
down. Don't push out at all. I'll catch you before you get
past me."

"Here I come!" Sister Cécile sounded almost as if she were laughing. She *was* laughing! She dropped and scrambled, and the man caught her and scrambled more. Together, they half climbed, half fell down the ladder. Surrounded by weeping, happy townspeople and most of the other sisters, they hugged and laughed and beat each other on the back. They completely forgot the burning church for a moment. They even forgot that one was a humble lay sister and the other a well-to-do merchant of the town.

Marie-Thérèse was busy trying to keep the children from dashing down the hill to join the triumphant crowd. She glanced toward the schoolroom as she grabbed the boldest of the little ones by the back of her skirt and yanked her further away from the fire. The flames, which had burned eagerly at the furniture and books and papers in the lowest floor of the main building, now arched hungrily upward. They reached the roof and climbed toward the cupola and then ran up the sides of the cupola. Nearby, the fire crawled up the church spire in yet another search for fuel. Marie-Thérèse watched, both fascinated and horrified. The spire burned like an enormous candle. Then the entire "candle" began to waver. There was an ominous rumbling sound.

"Get back, everyone! Get back!" Marie-Thérèse yelled at the top of her lungs. "Get back! The spire is falling!"

Slowly, gracefully, the spire shortened, shifted, and then fell, collapsing across the church roof. The pine beams that supported the roof already were on fire from the heat of the flames below them. While the bucket brigade stood helpless, the spire burned through the roof and plunged into the church itself, landing just where Marie-Thérèse, Anne, Al-soom-se, and the others had knelt less than an hour ago.

❧ 4 ❧

The Feast of Ste. Ursula

The old ash tree was still there, standing straight and tall just as it ever did. And, just as they had the day before, Marie-Thérèse, Anne, and Al-soom-se sat around its base and leaned back against its trunk, warmed by the late afternoon sun. Marie-Thérèse traced the grooves in the gray bark with one finger. She drew the same line over and over and over. She was so tired she felt as if someone had beaten her with a stick. "I wish I was with *les petites* about now," she said aloud. Even though it was broad daylight, Mother Mary had given orders that the little ones were to be given food and then put to bed at the Jesuit hospital. With food in their stomachs they would sleep. By the time they woke, plans would have been made to keep them busy and out of the way. The most important thing to do now was to clean up after the fire. Classes could wait. "I wish we all could go to bed, too—and forget this," Marie-Thérèse muttered. "When we woke up, maybe it'd seem old and over and finished. I know I could deal with it better if I could just get away from it all—just for one little minute."

Anne coughed. All three girls were sniffling and sneezing from the heavy smoke that still hung in the air. Shouts came from the far end of the monastery grounds as Jesuit priests and men from the city worked to knock down the remaining walls of the church and chapel. Immediately on the other side of the ash tree, the girls could hear lighter voices and a kind of scurrying. Standing on the far side of the monastery garden, Madame de la Peltrie's house was the only building of any size that had survived the fire. The nuns were hurrying to turn it into a temporary convent.

"It's funny, you know," Anne spoke up. "That house has never really been anybody's house. I know it was rented out for a while when it was new, but none of the nuns lived there. The bishop stayed there once, but he was only visiting. The only time anybody from the monastery has really lived in it is when something has burned down."

Al-soom-se sat up straighter. "You mean something burned before?"

"Mm-mm," nodded Anne. "The whole monastery burned in 1651, too. There are sisters here now who have had to move to that house both times—Mother Athanasius and Mother St. Ignace and Mother St. Croix have done all this twice."

The girls huddled back against the tree, thinking of what it would be like to lose everything to fire, not once, but two times. Would it be comforting to move back into the same shelter both times, or would it be scary? "Why did the monastery burn the last time?" Al-soom-se wondered. "Does anybody know?'

"It started in the kitchen then, too," Anne replied. She had spent a long while talking to Mother Mary of the Angels. The tragedy affected each nun, each pupil in different ways. Mother Mary had spent much of the day closer than ever to her students—talking to them almost as if they were her family.

Al-soom-se and Marie-Thérèse looked up, waiting for Anne to go on.

"I don't know who it was, but one of the nuns was baking bread. It was winter and cold in the kitchen, and the bread dough wasn't rising fast enough. So she put a pan of coals underneath the bread trough to warm it a little. Then she forgot what she'd done and went to bed. The coals set fire to the pinewood bread trough. The whole place burned—just like now. At least we've got good weather this time. That time it was in the middle of the winter. I guess the nuns ended up kneeling in the snow making a wall around *les petites* to keep them warm."

"Madame de la Peltrie's house can't possibly hold everybody," Marie-Thérèse changed the subject. "I helped in there once when it was being used as a schoolroom for the day students. Even if you covered the floor with people, there wouldn't be enough room for everybody to sleep."

"I asked Mother Mary about that too," Anne went on. "She says eight of the nuns will stay in the house for now—just enough so that the monastery will be occupied. She thinks they'll be able to get everybody in if they change things around. And they're going to fix up one of the stables to be a chapel, she said."

"What about us?" wondered Al-soom-se. "What will the other nuns do tonight? What about the Feast of Ste. Ursula?"

"She didn't really say about us. Tonight I guess we're supposed to go over to the Hôtel Dieu with the little ones. That's where the sisters who don't stay here will sleep. As far as the Feast of Ste. Ursula is concerned. . . . Well, they've cancelled the pageant because all our costumes and everything burned. There's still going to be a high mass tomorrow morning. Bishop Saint-Valier will be here to make it special. After mass, Mother Superior and some of the other nuns are going by carriage to see the governor. They'll make their regular Ste. Ursula's day visit to the Château St. Louis just as if nothing had happened at all. I think they hope that Marquis and Madame Denonville will be impressed that everything has been put in order so quickly. If the governor is impressed, I guess maybe he'll help pay for the rebuilding. Us? Well, you know they sent the day students home right away. We leave tomorrow, Mother Mary says—or as soon as our parents can come for us."

"Our parents . . . that's right! Oh, Marie-Thérèse! What will you do?" Al-soom-se stared at her friend.

"I'm not sure," Marie-Thérèse replied. "When my father brought me here in 1683, he thought I would leave the monastery only to be married. If I didn't marry, I could always keep house for him. With Mama dead, I think he almost wanted that. But now that he's dead too, I don't really have a place—unless I do stay and become a nun."

"There's your Uncle François," suggested Anne.

Marie-Thérèse almost grinned. "That'd be fun, all right!" François Guyon was young and daring—and handsome, as well. But she shrugged. "No. That wouldn't work. He's away all the time. Now he's talking about going into some kind of shipping business with a Monsieur Cadillac. They may be partners or something. It'll have to be my brother Michel—or maybe Jacques. Most likely it will be Michel, because he's married. Jacques was here today helping to fight the fire. He said I was to stay in the Hôtel tonight. I guess they'll send someone for me tomorrow. Michel's wife Annette doesn't like me much. She didn't want me to go back to school in 1685 when Papa died. She wanted me to give up on ever marrying and just be a nun. School costs money she'd rather spend on things for her house."

37

"Well, anyway, if you stay with Michel and Annette, you'll be here in Québec. We'll be able to see each other. That's good at least!" Anne brightened. "And Al says that she's been asked to stay at the Hôtel Dieu until spring to help with *les petites* who couldn't go home. We'll all be together . . . sort of."

❧ ❧ ❧

Madame Cadillac swallowed. There was a lump in her throat. She felt as if the fire had happened just yesterday instead of nearly 60 years ago. She remembered how tired and confused she had been that day—and how good it had felt to realize that her friends still would be close. She gazed around the Castelsarrasin courtyard, looking at everything at once—the children, the cobblestones, the windows and doorways facing the court. If she blinked fast enough, she wouldn't cry. The children mustn't see her cry.

"Don't stop, Madame! Don't stop," begged little René, pulling on her skirt. "See? The sun is still high. Tell us what happened next. Tell us about meeting Governor Cadillac!"

"All in good time, René. All in good time. . . ." A Carmelite nun glided smoothly across the courtyard toward them, balancing a cup of tea. Marie-Thérèse took it and sipped at it gratefully. "Ah, yes. *Merci*. Thank you, Sister. My throat dries when I talk so much."

The nun leaned forward quickly and spoke in Marie-Thérèse's ear. Marie-Thérèse shook her head and pushed the nun away gently. "No, no! I am not ready to go inside. Don't worry. I am not tired—only my voice, only my voice!"

She turned back to the children. "Now, René, where was I? Ah, yes. Things had to be sorted out very quickly after the fire. Winter was coming. Winters can be very cold in *Nouvelle France*. . . ."

❧ ❧ ❧

It took less than two weeks for a kind of order to settle over what was left of the monastery. Day classes were canceled, and all boarding students had been sent home until the chapel and schoolroom and dormitory could be rebuilt. Madame de la Peltrie's house had been renamed "the Convent of Ste. Ursula." Marie-Thérèse was right about the new convent's small size. The two-story building was just twenty feet wide and thirty feet long. The sisters put up

38

THE URSULINES. Ursuline nuns wore different habits according to their office and how long they had been nuns. Most of the nuns whom Marie-Thérèse knew looked like the woman at the far right in this picture. The nun at the left is holding a "reliquary," a box to hold saints' posses-sions—or even their bones. It was a reliquary much like this one that Sister Cécile rescued when the second monastery burned. ("Ursulines," in Braun and Schneider, eds., *Historic Costume in Pictures*. 1907. Reprint, New York: Dover, 1975. Reproduced by permission of Dover Publications.)

partitions and more partitions, dividing the space into tiny cubi-cles. Early in November, seventeen days after the fire, the convent was ready. All twenty-eight nuns and lay sisters marched in a pro-cession from the Hôtel Dieu to the convent. All twenty-eight of them moved into Madame de la Peltrie's house to live.

During that crowded winter, the sisters used every spare moment to sew new things to replace those lost in the fire. When they weren't sewing clothes for themselves, they embroidered fine linens to sell. The embroidery would help a little to pay for the costs of rebuilding. Long before spring, the stable-turned-chapel was ready to use. Almost before the last of the snow melted, the Jesuits helped the sisters build a temporary classroom. They put the shed-like building in the open space next to the ash tree. Day students came back to school, and classes began all over again.

Unfortunately, the day students did not return alone. They brought something along with them. In the spring of 1687, there was a measles epidemic in Québec. It wasn't long before a student came to class with an achy head and gritty eyes. By the time that student was sent home sniffling and coughing, another and another began to blink painfully in the sunlight. In just a few days, one of the teaching nuns dragged herself to mass with a bright red rash on her face and hands. In the tiny, crowded convent, it would be only a matter of time before all were terribly sick. And so the washhouse, which had managed to escape the fire, became an infirmary—a place for sisters with the measles to rest and sleep until it was safe to let them go back to the convent.

The pupils who were well enough were anxious to return to school, and the convent was eager to let them come. Each pupil in school meant that much more money for rebuilding. But so many sisters were sick. "What must we do?" Mother Superior asked Mother Mary of the Angels. "We can't afford to let the students miss class. Now they want to be here, but if we can't hold classes regularly, their parents may find things for them to do at home. There's always the risk they won't send them back to us again. Now, of all times, we don't want to lose the money their parents pay us for tuition. Could some of the older day students help you teach the young ones?"

Mother Mary thought for a moment. "I considered that," she said, "but I don't think it would work. The day students are not as advanced as boarders of the same age would be. They just haven't had as much time for study. But don't despair," she added quickly, as a shadow crossed the superioress's face. "I have an idea. I hope I am not sorry that I have had this idea. But there are three who could help us. I know of three advanced students who know not only the basic studies, but who can help us with the teaching of court manners. They are here in Québec, Mother Superior."

"Marie-Thérèse Guyon and her friends?" asked Mother Superior. "Is this wise? Are you certain it is appropriate?"

40

"No, I am not," replied Mother Mary honestly. "But I think they grew up a great deal last October. I think, too, that there is little for them to do at home. I believe they will provide us with a solution to our problem."

Mother Superior smiled. "Ask them then. We can but hope that God will curb their spirit of adventure—at least until the measles epidemic is done."

⚜   ⚜   ⚜

In a matter of hours, word made its way from the convent to Lower Town. By the next morning, Marie-Thérèse, Anne, and Al-soom-se were trudging across the monastery grounds, headed for the makeshift classroom. "Did you think we'd ever be back here again?" Anne asked.

"And back under the ash tree at that!" laughed Marie-Thérèse. "Well, someone has to teach the little ones. Mother Mary says she's going to keep a close eye on us, though. I don't think she is quite comfortable with the idea of letting us tutor without one of the sisters being there."

"I am GLAD she needs us to help, though," Al-soom-se said fiercely. "The sisters have done so much for me. I'm just glad, glad, GLAD there's something I can do for them."

"I agree," said Anne. "They really need us now. And besides, it's good practice for us—working with the little ones, I mean. It will help when we have little ones of our own."

"I'm just glad, glad, GLAD to get out of Michel and Annette's house," said Marie-Thérèse.

❧ 5 ❧
The Language of the Fan

"Don't drop that, now! I swear, you act more like a peasant than the daughter of a *bourgeois*. A merchant's daughter doesn't slam things around like that. *Mon Dieu!* We certainly paid enough money for the sisters to teach you better ways!"

"They taught us not to swear, at least, Annette. *'Mon Dieu,'* indeed. You sound like one of the *coureurs de bois*. I am being careful." Marie-Thérèse sighed impatiently and turned away from the box she was unpacking. Still kneeling, she glared at her sister-in-law.

The two girls were about the same age, but they could not have been more different. Tiny Annette Guyon was a perfect *bourgeois* wife. For her husband Michel, she kept a home fit for a duke—or for a successful Québec businessman. Her house was spotless and well ordered, furnished in only the best and newest fashion. A visitor from France would have found it hard to believe that the money that paid for Annette's lovely things came from trading with woodland people—with the Iroquois and Algonquin.

At the moment, Annette and Marie-Thérèse were unpacking the latest shipment of goods from France. Marie-Thérèse dove into each packing case with enthusiasm. They all stank faintly of fish and salt—like the ocean itself. The smell was enough to set her dreaming again—not of adventure in the wilderness this time, but of traveling by sea to the courts of France. She pulled a heavy, lumpy object from the middle of a crate and spun around with it. "This must be something special. It's the only solid thing under all that cloth."

"'All that cloth' is going to be my new ball gown. I hope it's not crushed. They didn't put it under anything heavy, did they?"

Annette hurried over to see for herself. A beautiful pale blue bro-cade fabric lay where Marie-Thérèse had pushed it aside. The bro-cade was folded carefully with softer cloth tucked into each fold to keep the silken fibers from breaking. "Well—that's all right, anyway," Annette breathed a sigh of relief. "But look what you've done. Whatever you have there was packed in raffia, too, and now you've got shredded fibers all over the place."

Marie-Thérèse was struggling with an extremely heavy object about the size of a large teapot. "Oh, but look, Annette," Marie-Thérèse said as she stripped off the final layer of wrapping. She held up her prize. She was too delighted to stay angry. "I think it's a clock!"

It certainly didn't look much like the tall golden brown col-umn that stood in the hallway. The hall clock was made mostly of wood. Even the flowers that decorated its sides were made of dif-ferent shades of wood laid together and polished smooth. That clock had a shiny metal face and used hands pointing to Roman numerals to show the time. The object that Marie-Thérèse had just unpacked was entirely metal, and it didn't have a face. At the top where a clock face should have been, there was a round ball. A thin neck held up the ball and some strips of shiny bronze that surrounded it. Below the neck, a fat column widened into an even fatter base. At the very bottom, a square of marble made the widest base of all and braced the clock so that it couldn't tip or wobble. That was interesting enough, but what delighted Marie-Thérèse was the round ball at the top. It wasn't just a ball; it was a globe—a map of the entire world. Around where the equator should have been, a wide metal band stuck out edgewise. Roman numerals on the top side of the band showed what time it was as the globe turned past each hour.

"Of course it's a clock. It's the very latest thing," Annette replied, looking at the clock more closely. "It is different, isn't it? Not quite as elegant as some—but something that you don't see every day—not even in Québec. Wind it and let's see if it runs."

"It's ticking already. I'm not sure what I did—twisted the globe, I think. Don't we have to set it someway?"

"We can do that later," replied Annette—not quite hiding the fact that she hadn't a clue how to set a globe clock.

Marie-Thérèse didn't mind. She was staring at the globe itself. There they were in Québec—at the place where the St. Lawrence River cut deeply into New France. She put one finger on the spot. There, well over on the other side of the globe, was France itself. A ship had crossed the ocean to bring the clock to Québec. She could still smell the salt odor that clung to the packing boxes. "What would it be like," she wondered aloud, "to travel on a ship like that?"

"A ship like what?" demanded Annette. "If you're through with unwrapping the clock, fold the wrappings and put them here."

"Is that the last of the boxes?" Marie-Thérèse asked. "If we're done, I need to get back to the monastery. Mother Mary is expecting me to help the day students with the Language of the Fan this afternoon."

"You'd be better off thinking of your own future than that of a dozen children," Annette scolded. "If you had a proper vocation you'd be studying scripture and preparing to enter the convent yourself. Think about it. It's certainly not likely you'll marry. You're sixteen years old now. Only an old man would marry a girl that old—and I don't think you want to marry an old man. We probably couldn't find one willing to marry you anyway. You're certainly pretty enough, but you've never really learned to be a lady. All the fancy airs and fan language in the world don't take away from the time you spend in the woods with that Abenaki girl."

"Al is showing me the plants her family uses to cure fevers. Isn't taking care of the sick supposed to be part of a wife's duty?" snapped Marie-Thérèse, stung. "Anyway, I'm leaving now." The heavy door to the street made a solid "thump!" as she stomped out of the house.

She was still angry when she reached the monastery gate. She barely muttered "hello" to the porteress and swept on toward the ash tree.

"Oh my, here comes a storm," Anne greeted her. "Better not let Mother Mary see you looking like that. You're supposed to be teaching the girls to be ladies today."

"Don't you start! I've had about enough of that lately." Marie-Thérèse rummaged through the shelves by the schoolroom door. "Where's my fan? I know I left it here after yesterday's class."

"Here you go," said Anne. "I was practicing with it in case you didn't make it and I had to teach the lesson. Is that it? They don't think you're a lady?"

"Worse than that," Marie-Thérèse replied. "Annette is really pushing me to join the convent. Like now. They're probably right that I won't get married, but there has to be something else I can do besides be a nun."

"What would be so bad about that—I mean, if you don't want to get married and have children?" Anne wondered. "The sisters are happy. They don't work any harder than you'd have to work to keep up a house, and the lay sisters help the way servants would in a fine home. There's plenty to eat, and you could go right on teaching. I think you like working with the little ones."

"Oh, Anne. Don't you understand at all? I don't want to stay in one place all the time! If I were back in Paris, I might want to follow Marie de l'Incarnation here to New France. That would be adventure. But here, well, about the only adventure the sisters have had in almost forty years is being burned out twice! I want to see the places Al-soom-se has been. I want to see the great falls in the land of the Huron. I want to see places nobody has ever seen—not even the Abenaki. I don't want to be a nun. I'm too old to marry, Annette says. Well, I'm too young to be a nun. I'm not ready to be a nun!" Marie-Thérèse stormed out of the schoolroom door, heedless of anyone who might be on the other side. She plunged straight past Mother Mary of the Angels, almost bowling her over.

Anne followed Marie-Thérèse to the door. The first thing she saw was Mother Mary dusting the folds of her habit. "What in the world is the matter?" Mother Mary asked, ducking as Marie-Thérèse returned almost as rapidly as she had left.

"Excuse me, Mother." Marie-Thérèse snatched the fan that Anne held out to her. Then she was gone again.

"What has happened?" Mother Mary asked again.

"It's her sister-in-law, and I guess her brother, too," Anne replied. "They are always telling her that she has ruined her chances to be married and that she should give herself to God instead. But she doesn't want to be a nun."

"So I gathered," said Mother Mary dryly.

Marie-Thérèse hurried across the grass toward her pupils. They were grouped together in a patch of spring sunshine, awaiting her arrival. It was easier to smile when she saw the eager faces before her. Everyone enjoyed the Language of the Fan. It was like learning a secret code. By the time she stood before them, Marie-Thérèse was ready to have fun, too. She closed her fan and held it in front of her with her left hand, touching its tip with one finger of the other hand. "What am I saying?" she asked merrily.

"You want to speak to us!" "I want to speak to you!" "It means you want to talk to us!" "You want to get to know us!" the voices chorused.

"Very good," replied Marie-Thérèse. "Now when would you make such a gesture?"

This time the answers were slower in coming. "Maybe if you had a secret to tell?" one little one ventured.

"Maybe if you saw a handsome boy and wanted to get to know him better?" said another.

"Yes, that's it. But then you can do this, too . . ." and Marie-Thérèse opened the fan to its fullest and held it in her left hand. She lifted it to cover much of her face.

"I want to get to know you!" cried the first girl. "Show us another."

"All right," smiled Marie-Thérèse. "This is a new one. Can you guess what this is?" And she returned the fan to her right hand and turned so that the open fan covered her left ear.

"We don't know that one."

"Think!" said Marie-Thérèse. "What am I doing?"

"Covering up your ear," said a little girl named Brigitte.

"And what do you suppose that means, Brigitte?"

"Don't listen."

Marie-Thérèse shook her head.

"Don't let anybody else listen?"

Marie-Thérèse nodded. "That's close. It's 'Don't let anybody else know our secret!'"

And so it went. The Language of the Fan had as many "words" as there were gestures you could make with a fan. Over the voices and music of a dress ball, with a fan a lady could say almost anything she wanted to say. She didn't have to be unladylike and shout. More than that, she could say things she might not dare to say out loud. Touching the handle of the fan to the lips meant "kiss me." Marie-Thérèse hadn't taught the children the sign for "kiss me" yet. She remembered too well the giggles and horseplay that followed when that particular bit of code was taught to her own class!

The Language of the Fan was a kind of secret code, but the person watching had to know the same code. Here in New France, of course, they learned the Language of the Fan that was used in the court of Louis XIV, the great Sun King. But Sister Cécile, who had been a famous belle before she joined the Ursulines, once told

Femme de qualité en Stenkerke et falbala

A LADY OF QUALITY. Just as the men of Québec dressed like fine French gentlemen (see illustration p. 50), fine ladies in Québec waited for ships from France to bring news of the latest fashions. This print, dated about 1700, shows a lady wearing the very newest style in dress. Look very carefully at the way she is holding her fan. If the handle is touching her cheek, she's saying, "Yes." If it slips and touches her lips, she's saying, "Kiss me!" (J. du St. Jean, *Femme de Qualité en Stenkerke et Falbala*, Victoria and Albert Picture Library, G. 747.)

Marie-Thérèse, Anne, and Al-soom-se of a great joke on herself. She had been invited to an elegant ball at the Château St. Louis. There, she dropped her fan to say to a young man "We will be friends"—only to learn that, where he came from, the same gesture meant "I belong to you"—a declaration of undying love! "He was pretty startled, I can tell you!" Sister Cécile laughed. "We'd only just met!"

But the children loved the Language of the Fan, and here in Québec, all the young ladies were taught the same code. At last Marie-Thérèse turned away from the little group, her fan held high behind her head with one finger extended. "Good-bye, Marie-Thérèse," the children chorused. She repeated the gesture before turning to go back to the schoolroom, but this time with all her fingers together on the fan. "Don't worry. We won't forget you!" the children promised.

"Nor I, you," laughed Marie-Thérèse, hurrying across the green.

❖ 6 ❖
A Bit Like the Devil

Marie-Thérèse's black mood returned as she trudged from the monastery to her brother Michel's home in Lower Town. By the time she leaned on the front door to open it, the least suggestion would have sent her flying back up the cliff—not to join the Ursulines, but to run deep into the woods beyond the monastery and lose herself there.

"Is that you, Marie-Thérèse?" Annette's voice came from the back of the house. "We have the clock running. Come and see!"

Marie struggled to kick off the clogs she wore to protect her shoes from the street. Now where were her house slippers? Yes, she'd left them in the front room, preferring to do the morning's unpacking in stocking feet. She ducked across the hall into the great front parlor—and stopped. There, in front of the fire, sat a strange man. He was elegantly dressed in fine brocade, but his hands and face were tanned dark brown by sun and wind. Unlike most of the fine gentlemen of New France, he didn't have on a wig. He wore his own hair, but its black waves clustered as heavily around his face as the curls of any wide-bottomed peruke would have done. There was heavy lace at his throat and more lace at his wrists. The large, broad-brimmed hat resting on his knees was covered with ostrich plumes dyed saffron yellow to match his fine suit. Light from the fire flickered across his face, making deep shadows in the hollows of his cheeks and lighting up his narrow black mustache. He looked up idly toward the door. Behind Marie-Thérèse, Michel stepped in from the hallway and reached out to hand the stranger a mug of brandywine.

"I think you've frightened my little sister, Antoine." Michel sat down opposite the stranger and grinned up toward the doorway. "You do look a bit like the devil sitting there in the firelight."

Marie-Thérèse gasped. She suddenly realized she'd been staring at the stranger for a very long time. She ignored Michel's attempt to call her into the room, grabbed her slippers, and fled up the hallway.

Annette was waiting for her in the dining parlor. "There, there's the clock." She pointed toward the sideboard that stood against the wall beyond the banquet table. "Your uncle François set it for me."

"Uncle François? What is he doing in Québec?"

"He escorted his new partner here to meet with Michel. They're discussing some shipping venture or other." She paused. "Marie-Thérèse, did you think about what I said this afternoon? I know I was sharp with you, but we have to face facts. One of the reasons François came to see us was to be certain that Michel and I aren't holding you back on purpose. He was afraid that I was keeping you here just to help me around the house." Annette put a hand on Marie-Thérèse's arm. "You really must find a life of your own. I was overly harsh today. You could still marry, if only you'd not be such a tomboy. Any man you've ever met you have frightened away. If you haven't done something outrageous like carry in a fresh beaver skin, you've quoted Greek and Latin at him. You need to focus on the other things you've learned: the way to dance, the way to charm, the way to make a man feel that he matters. I really don't know what is the matter with you. You are so pretty. You don't look as old as you are. If you'd just try, you could have your pick of half the men in Québec. They would line up to ask for you in marriage."

Annette kept on talking, but Marie-Thérèse quit listening to her. Most of it she had heard before, though not quite with this sense of urgency. "It must be that Michel's business with Uncle François is something that makes it harder for them to keep me here," she thought. "Probably it's that I cost them too much money whether or not I go to school. I'll bet they have been asked to invest money in François's business." Thinking, she began to drift back out of the room toward the hallway. There was truth in al! that Annette was saying. She didn't need to be told it again. But she didn't want to marry any more than she wanted to be a nun. Both were things that would tie her to one place. Both meant the end of her dreams of traveling into the wilderness.

"Marie-Thérèse?" she heard Annette say.

Maybe teaching was the better thing to do. Maybe she should

Nobleman   Officer

A NOBLEMAN AND AN ARMY OFFICER. Even though it was in the middle
of the Canadian wilderness, by 1686 Québec was a thriving city. The
men who lived there, especially the ones who worked at the Château St.
Louis in Upper Town, dressed as elegantly as the men back in France
did. The army officer is in uniform, but he still has a fashionable bunch
of ribbons on one shoulder and an enormous ostrich plume (feather)
on his hat. ("Nobleman and Officer," in (Braun and Schneider, eds., *Historic
Costume in Pictures*. 1907. Reprint, New York: Dover, 1975. Reproduced by
permission of Dover Publications.)

talk to Mother Mary about being a nun. Maybe she could work in one
of the missions with the Jesuits. She was almost to the front door.

"Marie-Thérèse? Are you even listening to me? I take it all
back. I meant what I said this morning. You are impossible!"
Annette hissed at Marie-Thérèse's departing back. "Go to the
nuns, then. Tell them to take you off my hands. You are unnatural. You are not fit to be a wife!"

That was too much. Marie-Thérèse's temper boiled over. She whirled back from the door and advanced on her sister-in-law. "Unnatural, am I? Unfit, am I? At least I don't shriek at my husband like a screech owl if I don't get my own way. At least I don't spend all his business profit on silly clocks. At least I can tell the truth and admit that all this is about money. You want me to get married? All right. I'll marry that man in the front room!"

To her surprise, Annette laughed out loud. "He might be a match for you at that! But you'll not marry that one. That is Monsieur Antoine Laumet de Lamothe Cadillac, your Uncle François's new business partner. Monsieur Cadillac is an explorer and a merchant, but they say he is also a pirate—a privateer. He is ten years older than you are, and I doubt very much he has room for any woman in his life, much less a spoiled little girl who won't accept the responsibility of growing up."

Marie-Thérèse fled out the front door, Annette's laughter ringing in her ears.

The light was fading fast as she made her way back to the convent. The waiting porteress was startled to see her so late in the day. Marie-Thérèse was beyond pride. "I want to stay here tonight. May I see Mother Mary of the Angels—please?" she begged.

"Just wait here, dear. I'll fetch her for you." The porteress, one of the older *canadienne* nuns, knew trouble when she saw it. She hurried off, her stout figure rocking from side to side as she trotted in the direction of Madame de la Peltrie's house. In moments, she was back with Mother Mary and Al-soom-se.

Mother Mary opened her arms. When Marie-Thérèse emerged from their shelter, both she and Mother Mary were wet from her tears. "What must I do, Mother? I really don't want to be a nun. I think I'd rather marry a pirate at that!"

"You must go to sleep and rest. Things will seem better in the morning." Mother Mary beckoned to Al-soom-se. "Denise will take you with her to the Hôtel Dieu tonight. The two of you can help the hospital nuns this night. Come to mass at the stable in the morning. We'll talk then."

⚜   ⚜   ⚜

Huddled together under a single blanket (the hospital nuns had been a little startled to find themselves with two guests from the monastery instead of one) Marie-Thérèse and Al-soom-se talked well into the night. "The funny thing, Al, is that I can't stop thinking about Monsieur Cadillac. I think I really could marry him. I mean, it hardly would mean being tied to one place. And he's rich," Marie-Thérèse whispered.

"And he sounds good-looking, too," agreed Al-soom-se. "Do you think he heard you say you were going to marry him?"

That stopped Marie-Thérèse's breath for a moment. Then she thought about the argument. It had been a fierce one, but Annette hadn't raised her voice. That meant Marie-Thérèse probably hadn't, either. "I don't know," she answered. "But I really don't think so. Anyway, he and Michel were busy talking business. I think he saw me, though, before."

"You need to meet him properly in a better setting," murmured Al-soom-se. "And we need to learn more about him, if you are going to be able to say the right things when you do see him." She was silent. "I think you will meet him, though, and I think you are going to marry him."

Marie-Thérèse was so surprised by her friend's positive tone that she sat bolt upright in bed, pulling the cover off them both. "How can you sound so certain?"

"Lie back down here. I'm freezing. It's only May and it's still cold at night, or hadn't you noticed? I'm sure because I am sure. Because once long ago I had a vision of you standing by the water with a man with long black hair and a black mustache. You belong with this Monsieur Cadillac—you'll see."

Mother Mary said nothing in the morning, noting only that her wild charges came to mass looking at peace with themselves. "They look as if they have a purpose in life," she smiled to herself. "They are young. God will sort things out for them." Mother Mary already knew what Al-soom-se's purpose was—or was supposed to be. It would not be long before she would return to the Abenaki to teach her entire village of the ways of their French neighbors. "But what, I wonder, has changed for Marie-Thérèse since yesterday?" Mother Mary said to herself.

One thing had not changed, and Marie-Thérèse headed for the schoolroom to teach the morning class in the Language of the Fan. There wasn't time to explain everything to Anne before class. After class, Anne was kept in the schoolroom to hear *les petites* do their numbers. It was not until the noon meal, when the sisters were busy explaining the afternoon's lessons, that Anne and Marie-Thérèse could talk.

"You really mean it, don't you? You really want to marry this pirate. You've never even spoken to him, Marie-Thérèse! How can you be so sure?"

"It's just like Al said last night," Marie-Thérèse answered soberly. "I'm sure because I'm sure. I just know this is right. I knew it when I told Annette I would marry him. At first I only said so because I was mad. But as soon as I heard myself, I knew it would happen. But we have work to do first!" Her eyes twinkled. "The three of us are going down to Lower Town this afternoon, and this time we aren't going to get in trouble for it."

Marie-Thérèse, Anne, and Al-soom-se made up a very different group from the one that had used the long staircase to go to Lower Town the last October. But just as they had done on that October day, the three headed briskly toward the waterfront. This time they turned aside well before they reached the busy docks. They walked down a street of shops and tearooms. "There is where we are going," said Al-soom-se, pointing. "Uncle Pierre said he would wait for us in the Cape Breton Tea Room. He's staying with Monsieur Cadillac; they are both guests of the governor at the Château. But I didn't think we wanted to meet him there."

"Uncle Pierre?" asked Anne. There'd not been time to bring her up to date on everything.

"Yes," replied Al-soom-se. "The explorer Pierre Roy is my uncle. He married my aunt. She died, but he is still my uncle and he recognized me when I went to see him today.

"Everyone knows that Monsieur Cadillac does a great deal of business at the Château St. Louis. When Marie-Thérèse told me about seeing him at her brother's house, I remembered that Uncle Pierre also did business with the governor. So—I hurried my chores at the Hôtel Dieu this morning and went to find Uncle Pierre." Anne and Marie-Thérèse looked at each other. That had to have been quite a task all by itself.

"Anyway, Uncle Pierre agreed to tell us what he knew of Monsieur Cadillac. He laughed at me. I think he thinks it's all a great joke on Monsieur Cadillac. But we don't care what he believes—as long as he tells us what we need to know."

❧ 7 ❧
Soldier / Spy?

The Cape Breton Tea Room could be identified by the large blue wooden teacup swinging from a bracket over its door. Otherwise, it looked much like the low shop buildings on either side of it. Its front was finished stone, but most of the building was of the same pine that made Lower Town merchants so afraid of fire. The Cape Breton had two large windows that opened onto the street. Between its windows, a door stood open wide. Through the door, the girls could see far enough into the dim interior to make out fine chairs and people in them leaning forward to talk to each other. In the very back of the room, several men gathered about a card table to watch others play a game of whist. Maybe because of the spring sunshine, someone had pulled benches out into the street and placed them under both windows. On one bench, a short, dark-haired man in an everyday suit of brown cloth sat watching the street. As he saw three young ladies approaching him, he stood, swept off his wide hat with its plain white feather, and bowed with a great flourish.

"*Bonjour, Mesdemoiselles*—my fine ladies!" No one could call Pierre Roy handsome, but his eyes twinkled and his smile was warm. "I'm not dressed to mingle with that fancy lot in there," he gestured over his shoulder, "but they will let me come in if I'm accompanied by such elegant women."

"Oh, let's stay out here, Uncle Pierre. The day is far too nice to spoil it by being indoors." Al-soom-se spoke from her own desire to stay in the sunshine, but Marie-Thérèse and Anne were quick to agree. Tugging and pulling the second bench to face the first, they sat down on it with their backs to the street, facing Pierre Roy the way pupils in a class face a teacher.

"Perhaps I should have said 'amazons' instead of 'fine ladies,'"

Pierre Roy laughed at the ease with which Marie-Thérèse moved the heavy bench. "Don't tell me. You—the tall one. You must be the one so anxious to know about Monsieur Cadillac."

Marie-Thérèse blushed. Until that moment, she hadn't realized she could blush, and she was furious with herself. Anne spoke up quickly.

"Monsieur Roy," Anne began with a glance toward Marie-Thérèse. Marie-Thérèse had stood up to hide her blush and was walking toward the open door of the tearoom. "Monsieur," Anne repeated, "Marie-Thérèse expects to be introduced to Monsieur Cadillac soon, and she must know more about him. It is important that she be able to talk with him easily. She does not want him to think that women in her family are empty-headed and vain—as he must think if he meets her sister-in-law Annette. You know that Monsieur Cadillac is in business with Marie-Thérèse's uncle, and now perhaps with her brother as well. But it is for that reason that they do not talk about him at home. Michel Guyon feels that women do not need to know about anything that has to do with business."

"That could be his loss," Pierre Roy said dryly. He had tried in vain to attract the busy serving girls who carried pots of tea and teacups to teashop patrons. Now, within moments of her arrival, Marie-Thérèse somehow not only had ordered tea but had managed to have it brought outdoors—where teapot and cups now sat on a tray, steaming slightly in spite of the warm air.

Feeling more dignified with a teacup in her hand, Marie-Thérèse turned back to Pierre Roy. "Yes, please tell us all you can. We haven't much time today, and so we must be rude and ask to be told—rather than try to get the same information from you through pleasant conversation. I am very anxious to make a good impression on Monsieur Cadillac when we meet."

"I don't think you will need to know much about Antoine for that to happen," Pierre Roy began, and then continued rapidly when the expression on Marie-Thérèse's face turned to one of dismay. "But I'll be pleased to tell you what I can. You are lucky. Antoine and I have been struggling to find things to talk about other than who discovered what piece of wilderness first. Last night we talked at length about France—and home.

"Antoine's name used to be just 'Antoine Laumet.' He was born in 1658 in the south of France in a place called St. Nicolas-de-la-Grave." Marie-Thérèse and Anne looked at each other. This made Antoine twenty-eight years old, twelve years older than Marie-Thérèse. "St. Nicolas-de-la-Grave is not far from the Pyrenees Mountains. Antoine has Spanish blood, you know—and sometimes I think that explains a lot about him. He is very conscious of rank, of being better than some kinds of people. Yet he is warm, and outgoing, and he loves his music."

"Antoine's parents died in 1677. He didn't say why—perhaps of disease, perhaps they were just old. But that is when he went into the army. He entered as a cadet, got himself promoted to lieutenant, and if he needs to impress you, he'll probably tell you that he was made captain as well. But just between us," Pierre Roy winked at Marie-Thérèse, "I think he was lucky to have been made lieutenant. He can be a wild one! He was still in the army—a proud member of the Clairambault Regiment—when he came to *Nouvelle France* three years ago."

"If his name was Antoine Laumet, where did the 'de Lamothe Cadillac' come from?" Al-soom-se wondered.

"Our Antoine needed style," grinned Pierre Roy. "Not everyone who joins a regiment is promoted. Not everyone gets to come to the New World. Antoine needed to sound as if he already was somebody—to attract attention, you understand. He needed a title. So he made one up. Is that so terrible?" Anne and Al-soom-se looked slightly shocked. People could be hung for pretending to be aristocrats. Marie-Thérèse was fascinated. A pirate? An adventurer? And now Antoine Laumet de Lamothe Cadillac had turned out to be a man with a false name? She knew she should be alarmed, but something told her there was no real harm in this.

"Our Ursuline nuns take the names of saints in order to be more like them. I don't suppose what Monsieur Cadillac did was that different. But where did he get the name?" Marie-Thérèse wondered aloud.

"'Lamothe' comes from *la motte*—the hill. There was a hill near his village. What can I say? Besides, he is distantly related to the de LaMothe family. Some say he is related to the Cadillacs, too. He told me he always liked the countryside where the village of Cadillac used to be. I think he didn't dare make an outright claim to the name LaMothe, but to be a Lamothe Cadillac? That is something different. He uses the de LaMothe coat of arms though. He has colored parts of it a bit differently, but it is the same coat of arms."

"What happened after he came to New France?" demanded Al-soom-se. "Come on, Uncle Pierre. You know the kind of stories that are told about him."

"Ah, well. I can't be too harsh in my judgment of him, because somewhere along the line he impressed the people at court. He came here on a secret mission for the king himself. Perhaps Louis liked him because he is so open, so honest. Antoine has no time for the fancy manners of court. He will tell Louis exactly what he learns in New France—never mind who might want him to say something different!

"Anyway, what he does here continues to be partly secret. They call Antoine Cadillac a pirate, but it is the English to the south who say "pirate" the most. He is a privateer. If he stops a ship or takes something that maybe does not belong to him, he does it for the crown. I don't know if he has letters of marque— an official license to be a privateer—but I can promise you that pirates are not entertained at the Château St. Louis as is our Antoine.

"Louis XIV wants to explore as much of this new world as he can, and he needs honest young men to explore for him. He needs people to tell him the truth about others who are trying to take the land that is part of *Nouvelle France*—New France. Antoine watches the English for Louis. I think maybe he watches the French, as well. I think even some days he watches me!" Pierre Roy laughed, and the girls laughed with him.

"So, does this mean that he is only a visitor to New France? Will he go back to Paris and the king and live in France when he's found all he's been sent to find?" Marie-Thérèse wanted to know.

"Jamais! Never! At least not soon!" Pierre Roy was more certain of that than anything else he had told them. "Not that one. He does not like to stay always in the same place. He wants to see things no one else has seen." Here, Anne nudged Marie-Thérèse so hard she gasped a little for breath. But she grinned at Anne. This was sounding better and better.

Pierre was still talking. "Antoine will build and make a place for others to follow him, but he wants more than anything to open new country—to make money through exploration. He talks all the time to the Huron and the Abenaki—even to the Iroquois. He wants to know about the lands to the west of here— as much for himself as for the king, I think.

"But he will stay in New France as long as he can. Just last night he was talking about how he soon would need to find a wife to help mind his property in Port Royal. He's a wealthy man there, you know. He owns many miles of land granted him by the king. But he is like any other man. He wants sons to carry on his name. He tells me that he thinks it will be hard to find a lady who is willing to marry a privateer—and he wants to marry a lady. I said last night that he would have to pay many blankets to find a squaw willing to put up with him! But maybe I was wrong?" Once again Pierre Roy laughed merrily. Marie-Thérèse blushed again, but she, Anne, and Al-soom-se could not help joining him. Pierre Roy pointed to Marie-Thérèse's reddening face, and they laughed the more, leaning against each other for support.

❧ 8 ❧

Making Plans

It was harder to find private time to meet at the ash tree now that the schoolroom was nearby, but it still was the quietest place to sit and talk.

"Now what?" demanded Marie-Thérèse to Al-soom-se. "Antoine Laumet de Lamothe Cadillac isn't a pirate, but he is a privateer. He's an explorer and an adventurer, and now we know that maybe he's a spy. He's twelve years older than I am and he's looking for a wife. But he's not looking for me. He doesn't know I exist, and my good brother likely won't think to change that. Worse yet, it sounds as if Monsieur Cadillac and I think exactly alike about traveling into the wilderness, and I will never, ever get the chance to tell him so. And there's something else you don't know. Things got a whole lot worse this morning."

"How is that?" asked Al-soom-se. "Something will work out. You'll see. It just has to. We only have to put our minds to it. Now think. Where can you go to be introduced to him?"

"You weren't listening. You didn't hear what I just said. It's not just 'where,' it's 'will there be time,'" mourned Marie-Thérèse. "Did you see me talking to Mother Mary this morning?"

"Yes. Neither of you looked very happy, so I didn't interrupt."

"We weren't happy, either of us. You know, it's funny. Since the fire, Mother Mary acts more like a friend than a teacher. I think maybe it's because she's known us all so long, and during the fire we were in trouble together and had to depend on each other. At least she knew me well enough this morning to know I wasn't going to like her news. She says Michel went to see Mother Superior yesterday. He's offered her a huge dowry for me—lots of

59

money as a gift to the monastery—if the sisters will just take me off his hands. He knows Mother Superior needs money right now because of the fire, and he figured that since I already was helping with *les petites,* she'd be really glad to take me as a nun. Mother Mary heard the whole thing through those thin walls in Madame de la Peltrie's. She told me that Mother Superior explained to Michel that I didn't want to be a nun. That didn't make any difference. Then Mother Superior tried telling him that it requires hard work and great love to be an Ursuline—that it wasn't something that could be chosen for another person. I would have to come to it myself. Michel just said he'd see that I 'came to it.' Finally Mother Superior looked at all that money and promised to take me as a novice. She asked Mother Mary to tell me the good news. Mother Mary said to pray about it—that God would help me in his own way. She made it really clear that, if and when I take my final vows as a nun, the decision will be mine alone—and I guess Mother Superior said the same thing to Michel. But by then it'll be too late to make any difference." Marie-Thérèse was almost in tears.

"Well, you're not a novice yet," soothed Al-soom-se. "And you can't be one if you are going to get married instead. We've just got to get you married. Michel should be glad to let you marry. You'd be out of the house just the same as if you were a nun. Couldn't you get him to introduce you to Monsieur Cadillac?

"Marie-Thérèse nodded, then shrugged. "Yes, I guess he would. But I don't think he'd see it as a way to get rid of me. I think it would be more of the 'You've frightened my little sister' thing—just sort of a joke. Michel wants me to be a nun because I'm too independent to be his idea of a wife. I'm sure he thinks all men would agree with him—especially older men like Monsieur Cadillac. I wonder why he thinks I'd be any better with the sisters.

"And whatever you say—Michel will never introduce me to Monsieur Cadillac as a potential wife because he thinks I'd insult him or something, or do something really crazy. I'm pretty sure that he'd be afraid I'd make his new business partner angry. Remember when Annette was scolding me the other day? She was still thinking of the day I traded for a fresh beaver pelt of my own—and brought it into the house right when she was about to introduce me to the brother of one of her friends."

Al-soom-se wrinkled her nose.

LES MOYENNES AND LES GRANDES. The Ursulines ran another school, the *Maison Royale de Saint-Cyr*, in France. All four of these girls studied there. The students in the first picture are about the same age as *les moyennes* (the "middles") in Québec. The third and fourth year students in the second picture are *grandes*—almost ready to be married. All these St. Cyr girls are from noble families and are dressed very, very elegantly. ("Girls of the 1st and 2nd Classes" and "Girls of the 3rd and 4th Classes." *Histoire de la Maison Royale de Saint-Cyr*. T. Levalée, 1856.)

"I guess it did smell pretty bad," Marie-Thérèse admitted with a rueful grin.

"So, what else can we do?" asked Al-soom-se. "It's not like you to give up."

"I thought maybe . . . somehow . . . that Pierre Roy would suggest something. But of course when we saw him, we acted as if it were all set—as if it were all planned for me to meet Monsieur Cadillac right away," Marie-Thérèse despaired.

"We agreed that we had to do that," All-soom-se nodded. "It would be too big a joke if we were counting on Uncle Pierre for an introduction. You saw what his sense of humor is like. It would be worse than Michel's treating you as a child. Uncle Pierre wouldn't mean any harm, but he could make the whole thing awfully embarrassing. Come on. THINK! What else?"

"What do you think I've been doing?" Marie-Thérèse asked a little irritably. "The only thing I can come up with is something that won't happen. Monsieur Cadillac is staying at the Château St. Louis. He'll be at Governor Denonville's spring ball. All I have to do is go to the ball. As if it's something I can just do, right?"

"Well you know all the dances. That wouldn't be a problem," Al-soom-se said helpfully. "All we need to do is get you in the door."

"I can't go to a ball unchaperoned. Nobody does that. Michel and Annette would have to take me, and they never will—not without some good reason. We're right back where we started."

"Here comes Anne. Maybe she's got a magic way to get you invited to the Château." Al-soom-se could see Anne hurrying toward them from Madame de la Peltrie's house. Work was already planned for a new hall to replace the one lost in the fire, but for now the small house still served the nuns as both home and meeting place. From the expression on her face, it looked as though Anne's meeting there had been an upsetting one. Fists clenched and arms pumping as she ran, Anne hurried toward the ash tree. Once there, she hurled herself down next to them, hitting the ground with a thump.

"You'll never guess," she said. "Madame Denonville's master of music has the measles!"

"So?" asked Marie-Thérèse, unhappily and a little rudely. "I mean, so does half the town still. Some have died of it. I'm sorry that the man is sick, but why do you care about him more than another?"

"He was supposed to play for the Governor's spring ball, that's why. And now they have only the members of the orchestra to play. There is no one there who can play the harpsichord well enough to suit Madame. Madame Denonville came to Mother Superior to see if one of the sisters would play, but of course that was not really considered. Instead, they've asked me to do it. I'm the best of the pupils, Mother Superior said . . . better now that I've practiced than even Mother St. Esprit. Now they are busy figuring out how to get me to the ball properly chaperoned. They didn't even ask me how I felt about playing in front of the governor and all his fancy guests."

Al-soom-se and Marie-Thérèse looked at each other. Then they fell on Anne laughing and shouting. "You did it! You had the magic wand! You are wonderful, do you know that? It's all going to work!!"

"Huh? What?" asked Anne in utter bewilderment.

"We'll go with you," said Al-soom-se, catching her breath. "Marie-Thérèse needs to go to the ball, and so we'll be your chaperones!"

"That's no good," objected Anne, only half understanding. "We'd just be three unchaperoned girls instead of one unchaperoned girl."

"Not if we went in the company of Michel and Annette, and they'd have to take us if the sisters asked," cried Marie-Thérèse in triumph. "Michel really wants to impress the sisters just now. This will work! It will! What have you told Mother Superior?"

"That I'd play, of course, but they were going to talk to Father Rafaix when he comes today to help on the new building. They thought he or the other Jesuits would know the best way to get me there."

"Let's go," said Al-soom-se, brushing off her skirts and pulling Marie-Thérèse to her feet. "Who is supposed to talk to Father Rafaix?"

"Mother Mary of the Angels," replied Anne.

"Better and better," grinned Marie-Thérèse. "But we need to talk to her first!" She and Al-soom-se hauled the still-puzzled Anne along with them. Hurrying back along the path to the convent, they hastily explained the situation. It didn't take Anne long to be almost as excited as Marie-Thérèse and Al-soom-se were. By the time they were at the convent door, she greeted Mother Mary with a radiant smile.

"Outside, girls," Mother Mary said, rising to meet them. "You look like you have much to say, and this house with its thin walls may not be the place to say it. I would not have you hide from God. But there's no need to tell Mother Superior what you are plotting until I have heard it first. And yes, I can see that you are plotting something. Two of you were in tears earlier today, and now you look like the sunshine on Easter morning!"

The four walked slowly back toward the ash tree. Marie-Thérèse, Anne, and Al-soom-se were silent, trying to decide how much to tell the older woman. Mother Mary was quiet, too, praying grimly and silently that she would manage to do the right thing for this worrisome trio.

The schoolroom had emptied while the girls were talking, so they went inside. Doing so seemed better than asking Mother Mary to sit on the grass. It kept things more certainly private, too.

Anne spoke first. After all, it was she who needed a chaperone. She sketched out the basic plan, and then added, "If we all go, it'll help another way. I won't mind so much having to play for all those people if Marie-Thérèse and Al . . . excuse me, Mother . . . and Denise are there."

"We'll need practice on the dances," admitted Marie-Thérèse. "But if we are seen to dance well and represent the school well, perhaps even more parents will want to send their daughters here. That will mean more money to help with rebuilding."

When it was Al-soom-se's turn to speak, she looked steadily at Mother Mary of the Angels. "You know, don't you, Mother? You know that, although we are telling you the truth, there is more to tell."

Mother Mary's voice was calm. "Yes, I could tell that there was more to the story. But I can wait for you to tell me what it is."

Marie-Thérèse put a hand on Al-soom-se's arm to keep her from speaking. This part of the story she had to tell herself. "Mother, you know I love you and admire you, but you also know that I do not want to be a nun."

"You've certainly made that clear enough," smiled Mother Mary.

"I'm not sure I can be a wife and mother, either, but I must be one or the other. I think I would be better as a wife."

"I have thought as much," agreed Mother Mary, "but you must know that it is not only the Ursulines that have rules. A husband will require you to be obedient also. And I believe that even the men of New France will not want a wife who prefers the woods to the parlor. We have taught you to run a house, to dance, to charm, but you do not take pride in the things you have learned. You still want to play in the woods like a child. Where do you expect to find a husband who will overlook this?"

"There is a man who would, Mother, or I think there is!"

Mother Mary of the Angels was forty-eight years old and beginning to feel her age. But she had taken her vows and become an Ursuline sister just fifteen years earlier. For thirty-three years, she lived in the world, and in Paris at that. She remembered very well what it was like to be young, and to dream. She knew how dangerous it was for young dreamers to confuse dreams with reality. She listened to Marie-Thérèse and knew that the man she was describing was said to be far more than just a privateer. Mother Mary even had heard it said that he had taken the name "Cadillac" because of some terrible scandal associated with the name "Antoine Laumet." She feared that she herself was committing a sin of omission when she did not roundly scold the three girls. After all, they had made yet another unapproved trip that took them far too close to Lower Town's wild waterfront. Everything the girls were telling her now could not be real at all, she thought. It was only a young girl's fantasy.

And yet it made perfect sense. "God moves in mysterious ways, His wonders to perform," Mother Mary quoted softly to herself.

The girls had fallen silent, waiting to hear what Mother Mary would say.

"Well, Marie-Thérèse, Anne, Den . . . Al-soom-se," Mother Mary smiled at the stunned gratitude on Al-soom-se's face when she heard her Abenaki name. "I think the first thing we need to do is get a message to Michel Guyon that we will need his sister here at the monastery for the next few days. And then, my children, we had best get to work on the latest dances from France." She staggered slightly as all three girls threw their arms around her, knocking her veil and wimple askew as they planted enthusiastic kisses on her face.

❖ 9 ❖
Preparations

" A nd one, and two, and three!" Mother Mary's voice chanted out the time as Mother St. Esprit coaxed a lilting melody out of an old recorder. "Very lightly, ladies! Now take the gentleman's hand—that's Sister Cécile's hand, Marie-Thérèse. Now, just for a moment—no, wait, Marie-Thérèse. Take his hand just for a moment, and THEN you turn away! No, no! You are not supposed to be pulling him from a well! Just a touch of the fingertips is all. Now, try again . . . And one, and two. . . ."

Mother Mary of the Angels sighed. "Here. Watch me." She stepped forward to take Marie-Thérèse's place. "We want great poise and grace. You must make the dance the most important thing—make the gentleman feel grateful for the little moment that he walks with you, and then turn away—always elegant. Hold your head just so."

Marie-Thérèse tried not to giggle as the little nun walked through the intricate steps of the minuet. It felt strange to dance to the sound of an old wooden flute instead of the stronger rhythm provided by the harpsichord, but the monastery's harpsichord had perished with everything else in the fire. It seemed stranger yet to watch the sisters in their habits nodding and turning, pretending to be lords and ladies at a grand ball. The recorder gave a sudden squawk.

"I'm sorry," laughed Mother St. Esprit. "I can't blow and smile at the same time, and you do look a sight!"

Mother Mary stepped back from Sister Cécile. The lay sister was grinning broadly. One of the first to be asked to help with the renewed dancing lessons, she willingly left her heavier chores to seek out her brother—a young naval officer just returned from France. With his help, she had brought several new dance steps to Mother Mary's attention.

"God has given us this opportunity. There is nothing wrong with enjoying it," Mother Mary said sweetly to Mother St. Esprit. "Just as I enjoyed watching you when you tried the steps of the *contre-danse*—it was all the steps at the same time, as I remember?"

It was Mother St. Esprit's turn to smile at herself. "What can you expect, Mother Mary? The *contre-danse* began as an English country dance. If I was clumsy, it's only because I was pretending to be English!" And they all laughed merrily, students and teachers alike.

A sharp tug on her skirt drew Marie-Thérèse's attention. She glanced down to see tiny Rose de Lauson, the smallest of *les petites*, staring up at her somberly.

"Are you really going to the ball?" Rose asked.

"Yes, *chérie*," smiled Marie-Thérèse, squatting down so that Rose could see her better. "Isn't it exciting?"

Rose nodded. Then she took a deep breath. "Will you take your fan?"

This apparently was a very important question, so Marie-Thérèse pretended to think about it a little. "Yes," she finally said. "I think I should, don't you?" To her surprise, Rose's eyes filled with tears.

"Whatever is the matter here?" Mother Mary bent down to see. Rose sobbed all the harder. Puzzled, Mother Mary felt her forehead. There was no fever. Sometimes children coming down with the measles cried without reason, but not like this.

"You've got to tell us what's wrong, or we can't help," said Marie-Thérèse. "Is it something about my fan?"

"Yee—sssss," wept Rose. "I was practicing. I was practicing so I could show you when you came to class next time. Louise had my fan, and yours was in the schoolroom. And, and . . . I opened it—fast like you showed us? And I closed it again. And then I opened it—only . . ." and she started to wail again.

"What happened, Rose?" prompted Mother Mary.

"I—I opened it too fast and my hand jerked, and I threw it in the well!"

Marie-Thérèse looked at Mother Mary. "Not a problem," she mouthed silently to the frowning nun. "It's all right, Rose," she said hugging the child to her. "It's all right. That was only my school fan. I use it for practice, too. I have a lovely new one that matches my ball gown. I'll show it to you the next time we have a class in the Language of the Fan." And she rocked back and forth slightly, comforting Rose, whose sniffles were ending almost as suddenly as they had begun.

"It may be all right this time, Rose," said Mother Mary, straightening up. "But you know what you did that was wrong, didn't you?"

"Yes," a whisper. "I took something that was not mine and then I lost it."

"What should you do now?"

"Should I go work for Sister Cécile? That's what you always do to Marie-Thérèse when she gets into trouble." Little Rose felt better when she could make people laugh, but she didn't see why all the nuns and Marie-Thérèse thought that was so funny.

Marie-Thérèse was not surprised that one of *les petites* knew about the governor's ball. The whole monastery had become involved in the girls' preparations for it. Almost everyone agreed with Marie-Thérèse that, if she and Al-soom-se looked stylish at the governor's ball, it would encourage school attendance. Now that money was needed so urgently for rebuilding, anything that would bring in more students sounded like a good idea. Finally and above all else, the whole idea of the ball promised to be fun.

Some of the older nuns had objected, of course. For some, at least at first, it did not seem right for the sisters to be so involved in a party—even just in getting ready for one. Old Mother St. Croix was particularly distressed that so much attention was being paid to music and dance when the monastery was not yet rebuilt. "And sisters," she cautioned. "We are reminded not to be so concerned about things of this world. The fire and the epidemic were our lessons. Have we not learned from them?"

But Mother Superior overruled her. "We must be mindful of what is important to God, of course, but our work should always be joyous. And besides," she said firmly, "it is entirely true that we need the money that more pupils would bring. People have stayed away, thinking that since the fire we no longer can care for our students. God has given Anne Picoté de Belestre this opportunity to show all of Québec that the young girls who come to us become accomplished in society. It will remind people that the school is

LADY PLAYING A HARPSICHORD. This French lady is playing a parlor-sized harpsichord—smaller than the sort used with an orchestra. In 1686, all *canadienne* girls of good family learned to play musical instruments. As a matter of fact, so many *Canadiens* owned harpsichords that, in 1760 when *Nouvelle France* surrendered to England, English soldiers laughed about the French "packing up their harpsichords" and going home. (*Lady Playing a Harpsichord.* Late seventeenth/early eighteenth century French print.)

still here and operating normally. We must support Anne in this."

Only Mother Mary knew the most important reason Marie-Thérèse was going to the ball, but after Mother Superior approved the idea, all at the monastery joined in to help. It was a relief not to think about the fire or the measles epidemic or any of a dozen other worries. The sisters turned their best embroidering skills to the decoration of ball gowns. Those who were the most musical set themselves to learning the very newest dances. Not only would Marie-Thérèse, Anne, and Al-soom-se be prepared for the ball, but all *les moyennes* and *les grandes* would be taught each new step. Mother Superior herself approached Michel Guyon. To her satisfaction, she found him more than willing to escort three senior students to Governor Denonville's ball.

"He just thinks it's a good opportunity to show the sisters how hopeless I am in society," Marie-Thérèse confided to Anne and Al-soom-se when she was told about it, "but I don't care. If he thinks I'm hopeless, he'll leave us alone once we're there."

Practicing the dances themselves was almost easy. The girls had danced many times before, though never when doing the newest steps perfectly was so very important. Now, with Rose and the crisis of the fan taken care of, practice began again.

"An *allemande,*" said Anne to Marie-Thérèse, hearing a change in the recorder's tempo. "The *allemande* is the best dance for you to dance with him. You are together as partners all the time, and you can talk during the turns."

"I'll be lucky if I meet him for five seconds in a *contre-danse,*" hissed Marie-Thérèse, scrambling to her feet to replace Mother Mary where she stood waiting with Sister Cécile. Nearby, Al-soom-se held the hands of one of the older *moyennes.*

Mother St. Esprit was well over her fit of the giggles, and the recorder notes sounded clear and sweet. The partners stepped out in time, but now, instead of turning aside as they did in the minuet, the dancers joined hands and moved as one. First they faced each other, and then, hands linked overhead, twisted to stand back to back. As Sister Cécile freed one hand, Marie-Thérèse spun gracefully to face her, smiling as she had been taught. "That's it," laughed Sister Cécile. "You'll break my heart that way!" Again and again they turned, twisted, stepped out in a pattern, and faced each other, spiraling in graceful obedience to the music.

"Very nice, very nice," applauded Mother Mary. "Al-soom-se,

keep your hands closer together. Remember that your partner will be taller than you are, and he must raise his hands as well. Make it easy for him to reach you."

The shadows were reaching from the schoolroom to the ash tree before the dancers, tired and happy, decided that the latest steps were mastered. There was just one more day until the governor's ball.

Anne gave Marie-Thérèse a quick hug. "Don't look so worried. It will be all right, you'll see! We all have a feeling about this."

"So do I," replied Marie-Thérèse, "a scared one."

"I'm the one who should be scared," responded Anne. "I'm off now to practice on the bishop's harpsichord. It's the only one as large as the one the governor keeps at the Château. I wish it could be a little one like the one the sisters lost in the fire. The big ones are so much harder to play. I have to really pound on the keys. My fingers get so tired, I just know I'll make a mistake."

"You could build your strength by helping me fold clothes in the laundry," hinted Sister Cécile.

All three girls jumped. They had been so intent on their worries that they'd not seen her turn back toward them.

"Come on," repeated Sister Cécile, her head cocked on one side. "The washhouse is still being used as an infirmary, and I've two young ones in there with the measles. We'll have to work outside, and I know that won't bother Denise in the least." Al-soom-se ducked her head and grinned.

"Come help," Sister Cécile went on. "The work will be good for you. It's something that needs to be done and it will let you think about something else for a change. Besides, if you absolutely refuse to talk about anything else, there's time between now and compline for you to tell me what this is really all about. All I can get from Mother Mary is that she is praying for you!"

"I have to have my dress fitted before the service of compline, but I'll come now for a little," said Marie-Thérèse.

"And I," said Al-soom-se.

"And I," said Anne somewhat grimly, "am off to practice on the bishop's harpsichord."

❖ 10 ❖
The Governor's Ball

Marie-Thérèse, Anne, and Al-soom-se walked gingerly over the cobblestones. It seemed like a long way from the road to the Château. "I wish your brother had let the driver take the carriage all the way up to the door," muttered Anne. Marie-Thérèse agreed with her, but she understood the impatience that kept him from waiting in the long line of carriages full of arriving guests.

In the twilight, it was hard to see where to step. To make matters worse, it had rained that afternoon and their fancy slippers slid on the still-wet pavement. Behind the girls, Annette, wearing her new brocade ball gown, clung to Michel's arm for support. They heard her catch her breath as her foot caught between two cobbles.

At last the stone front of the Château St. Louis loomed before them. A great, long building, it had three main wings that reached out toward them. Each wing was as large and tall as a large house. The main building behind them was far larger. Marie-Thérèse counted no fewer than seven chimneys carrying smoke from the fires that had been lit to take the chill off the spring night. At either end of the main building, two additional, smaller wings, each only half the height of the great Château, faded off into the darkness. The Château itself was ablaze with light. Almost three dozen windows—there were that many just on the side of the building facing them—shone brightly. Candlelight spilled out from the ground floor into the courtyard, and the damp cobbles gleamed in small pools of light. Elegantly dressed figures came and went in and out of a central doorway. Liveried (uniformed) servants of the governor stood on either side of the doorway, standing as straight and tall as the carved wood columns beside them.

Several women could be seen just inside the door. The embroidery in their dresses glittered faintly in the light. Marie-Thérèse looked first at their dresses and then down at her own gown. On that count, at least, she didn't need to worry. Her dress was every bit as lovely as those she saw on the women in the doorway or walking the path ahead of her. Her bodice and overskirt were made of heavy dark blue silk that rustled grandly as she moved, its folds gleaming in the candlelight. Ribbons lifted up the overskirt and tied it back on the sides. The skirt itself made a sort of puff on each side of her waist before it doubled back to make the back of her dress even fuller. There, where it draped all the way to the ground, it was longer than it needed to be and followed behind her in a small train. Because the overskirt was held back so far on the sides, a great deal of her apron was showing, and that was all the better. The apron was the very palest blue silk, and the sisters had used darker blue thread to stitch rows and rows of embroidered flowers around its hem and up the middle to her waist. Ahead of her, she noticed several women whose full sleeves were gathered tightly to their arms in several places. It looked almost as if they had three or more sleeves on each arm. Marie-Thérèse smiled. Triple-puffed sleeves were last year's fashion. Her own sleeves fell smoothly from her shoulders, almost like the sleeves of a man's coat. At her elbows, they ended in lace as fine as any worn by the governor himself. The same lace made up row after row of ruffles all down the front of her bodice. Because the women in Paris were beginning to wear very high *frontages,* or headdresses, Marie-Thérèse had dressed her curls as high as she

THE CHÂTEAU ST. LOUIS. Tradition says that this is where Marie-Thérèse met Antoine Cadillac. This view looks toward the château from its courtyard. The cliff and Lower Town are behind the building. The building's formal rooms were palace-like and intended for very important government occasions. It was the perfect place to give a ball. (C. W. Jefferys, *Chateau St. Louis,* National Archives of Canada, C-069132.)

73

dared in front and framed them with a lace cap. The cap was edged with a touch of the same ribbon that held back her skirts. She tucked her hands into a tiny muff of dark blue silk trimmed with snow-white rabbit fur and still more of the same ribbon. The handsome new fan dangled from one wrist, held there by a silken loop. Oh, yes. There was no doubt about it. She was dressed well enough to attend the court of King Louis XIV himself. Next to her, Al-soom-se was equally grand. Her dark skin glowed against pale yellow silk and a froth of white lace.

"We do look fine, don't we?" whispered Marie-Thérèse. "Thanks to the news from Sister Cécile's brother, I believe we are dressed in later fashion than anyone here! But there are so many people! How will we ever find Monsieur Cadillac in all this crowd, much less meet him?"

"I'll manage," said Al-soom-se knowingly. "Don't you worry about that!"

Marie-Thérèse felt Michel's hand on her elbow, propelling her through the door into the brilliantly lit hall. "I have business to discuss with François," he said to no one in particular. "You'll be all right on your own." Annette, too, melted away to join the older women—probably in a discussion of fashion and the latest news from Paris.

A liveried servant came to claim Anne. "Madame Denonville would like to speak to you in her chambers," he said, bowing slightly. "She is unable to attend tonight, but has asked that you play for her privately before playing for the dancers." He turned to leave, obviously expecting to be followed. Anne gave Marie-Thérèse and Al-soom-se a wan smile and hurried after him.

Music and the sound of voices filled the room. Men and women were arranged in squares about the room, and violins and the lower-sounding viols were scraping out the rhythm of a *contre-danse*. The dancers whirled and met and bowed and turned and went back to stand in their squares again, watching as the next couple bowed and turned. Marie-Thérèse's foot began to tap all of its own accord. She hardly noticed when Al-soom-se was swept away in whirl of yellow and white to join the square nearest them. A burly trader, his embroidered woolen clothes contrasting with the silks and satins of the men who were gentlemen or merchants, appeared before Marie-Thérèse bowing awkwardly. She barely spoke as he pulled her with him to join in the dancing. Mechanically, she bent her head and moved lightly down a line of dancers to take her place. Gentleman after gentleman greeted her as the dance went forward. She nodded and joined hands and stepped and turned as the dance required, but without really thinking of what she was doing. She was far too busy scanning the room, searching for Monsieur Cadillac. At last, the trader who had first claimed her partnered her again, and the dance was over. She found herself back near the wall, standing with Al-soom-se and tapping her foot as before.

In the furthest corner of the ballroom, she noticed a small group of men clustered near the governor, all talking animatedly. Michel and Uncle François were there. Marie-Thérèse watched them idly. Michel said something to a man she couldn't quite see. Uncle François struck him on the shoulder and laughed. The man to whom Michel spoke laughed also. She could hear his laughter above the music. As she watched, he bowed exaggeratedly and turned to walk away. Marie-Thérèse caught her breath. She had missed Monsieur Cadillac before because, without realizing it, she had been looking for the same yellow satin he'd worn on his visit to Michel. This time, Monsieur Cadillac was clad in a coat of pale green brocade covered with silver embroidery. The coat was so long it reached almost below his knee-length breeches. Just enough of them showed that she could see that both the breeches and his hose were a silken silver gray. His shoes and the ribbon garters that supported his hose were as green as grass. Here was a gentleman of high fashion in every way, but—and Marie-Thérèse smiled to see it—he still had no time for a periwig. She watched as he pushed his hair back from his face impatiently and hurried toward the door—and outside.

Before Marie-Thérèse had time to feel disappointed, he was back—this time with his arm across the shoulders of someone she knew well. "Look, Al! It's Pierre Roy!" she whispered to Al-soom-se. As the girls watched, Pierre Roy said something to Monsieur Cadillac and then walked over to join the group in the corner. Monsieur Cadillac looked around him, turning from side to side. "What's he looking for?" hissed Marie-Thérèse.

"I think he wants someone to bring them drinks," replied Al-soom-se. Seeing no servant close at hand, Monsieur Cadillac turned toward a buffet table that was set against the far wall. "Leave this to me," said Al-soom-se suddenly, and darted out onto the dance floor.

She cut swiftly between the dancers, and, only barely out of breath, arrived at the buffet table moments before Monsieur Cadillac. *"Bonsoir, Monsieur!* Good evening, sir!" she smiled. "I am almost embarrassed to ask this," she said, smiling more so that it was obvious that she wasn't embarrassed at all. "But you are Monsieur Cadillac, are you not?" He bowed slightly in acknowledgment. "Monsieur, I am the niece of Pierre Roy. He has told me, as well as my friends at the Ursuline school, so much about you. We are quite honored to have someone here who is in the acquaintance of our good King Louis. My friend Marie-Thérèse Guyon is here with me tonight. She would be so pleased to meet you. Could you accompany me for a moment?" and Al-soom-se opened her fan with her left hand and waved it slightly as she backed away.

"Guyon?" Monsieur Cadillac muttered under his breath. He turned back toward his friends. Someone must have said something highly amusing, because Pierre Roy was almost doubled up in laughter. He waved vaguely in their direction, and turned to follow Al-soom-se as she wove past the dancers.

Marie-Thérèse watched them approach, the tip of her finger to her closed fan as she had been taught. "I would like to make your acquaintance," that meant. That certainly was true. Her heart was beating so hard she could feel its pounding in her throat.

"Mademoiselle Guyon?" Marie-Thérèse curtsied slightly—just barely low enough for the movement to be graceful. "I am pleased to make your acquaintance. I am Antoine Laumet de Lamothe Cadillac, very much at your service, ma'am. I understand that you wish to speak with me." Monsieur Cadillac stood there before her, bowing deeply and smiling.

Marie-Thérèse looked briefly for Al-soom-se, but she was nowhere in sight. Now that she had Monsieur Cadillac there in front of her, she had no idea what to say to him. Poised, dressed in the latest French fashion, using the language of the fan as best she knew, she heard herself say, "Will a privateering venture help or hinder your observation of the English, do you think?"

She was horrified at herself! What a thing to have come out of her mouth! In one sentence she'd accused him of being both pirate and spy! She opened her mouth to say something else, anything else, but was stopped by the expression on Monsieur Cadillac's face. He was not insulted. Far from it! He looked a little stunned. Then he threw his head back and laughed so loudly, the other dancers turned to look at him.

"Who exactly are you, Mademoiselle, that you know so much about my affairs?"

"I am the sister of Michel Guyon and the niece of François Guyon," Marie-Thérèse replied, thinking that neither Michel nor François would admit to being related to her after she had made such a fool of herself. She couldn't think of a way to undo what she'd already done, so she plunged ahead. "I know so much," she said, "because you do so many things I would like to do myself." In the background, the music changed tempo.

"You would like to be a privateer?" frowned Monsieur Cadillac.

"No, no!" Marie-Thérèse shook her head, and one of the carefully placed curls in her headdress slipped down over her forehead. "I would like to explore. Al-soom . . . My friend Denise's brother has been to the great waters to the west. I too would like to see the great waters. I would like to see a waterfall so broad that it is as wide as the horizon. I would like to go further, into the lands beyond, where no Frenchman has ever been, and do so myself—before anyone else has been there to see."

Monsieur Cadillac was staring at her. Of course he was staring. None of this was what she had been taught. Nothing of what she said was going to make him interested in her as a wife. They were right, Annette, and Michel, and all of them. She would never be a wife. She would never even be able to talk properly to a man. She had best resign herself to living with the Ursulines for the rest of her life. The music was louder now, and she could hear Anne playing the harpsichord.

"An *allemande*," remarked Monsieur Cadillac, still smiling broadly. "Come and dance with me. I think I would like to know more about the things you would like to do."

Spinning and turning through the steps of the *allemande*, Marie-Thérèse answered Monsieur Cadillac's questions as best she could, but afterwards she could not remember anything that she had said. She knew only that he seemed to be pleased by her answers, and that every time she tried to say something that turned the conversation properly back to him, he would ask her another question. Much too soon, the dance was over and Monsieur Cadillac bowed low. Then he was gone to join the men in the corner again. Marie-Thérèse was left to face Al-soom-se.

"Well?" demanded Al-soom-se.

"Oh, I don't know!" wailed Marie-Thérèse. "I did and said

everything wrong. Oh, I danced well, and I know I look very fine, but—Al, I practically called him a pirate!"

"Was that before or after he asked you to dance?" asked Al-soom-se practically.

"Before, but . . ."

"Well, then you are all right. Smile! He may be watching you." Al-soom-se glanced quickly into the corner, but Monsieur Cadillac had turned his back to them.

"I don't want to dance any more," said Marie-Thérèse. "Let's find something to eat and then sit with the older women."

"That's probably a good plan," murmured Al-soom-se. "I don't know why, but I don't want your Monsieur Cadillac to see you dance with anyone but him."

Annette was surprisingly cordial when she saw them approach. "You looked very fine, Marie-Thérèse, out there on the dance floor."

"Yes indeed. She certainly did!" One of the other women came over to stand with them. "There's not another girl here who wouldn't give away her best gown for a chance to dance with Antoine Cadillac, and there's not another girl here who had the chance!"

True to her word, Marie-Thérèse refused to return to the dance floor. Now, more than anything, she wanted to go home—to think about the awful things she had said and the surprising way Monsieur Cadillac had reacted to them. The evening dragged on. Annette paid them little attention after her first greeting, and Marie-Thérèse and Al-soom-se were left to listen and watch, lost in the music and their thoughts. At length, the last dance was finished, and Anne came walking tiredly toward them. Michel followed behind her, ready to escort them all back to the monastery. He and Annette would return to the Château to spend the night before going home.

"Well, that's that," said Marie-Thérèse to Al-soom-se as they walked out the door. "I don't know what I expected anyway—even if I hadn't said all those stupid things. I could hardly expect him to ask me to marry him in the middle of the dance."

Al-soom-se and Anne said nothing, but linked arms around Marie-Thérèse's waist. Behind them, Antoine Laumet de Lamothe Cadillac looked up from his conversation to watch the Guyon party leave. He continued staring after them out the door, a thoughtful expression on his face.

❖ 11 ❖
Monsieur Cadillac Comes to Dinner

Marie-Thérèse stared at the figure approaching her across the open ground of the monastery. While she was accustomed to receiving messages ordering her back to the house for one reason or another, never before had Annette bothered to deliver one of them to her in person. Yet here she came now, walking rapidly and ignoring the group of *les petites* who stopped in their tracks to gape at the strange, hurrying lady.

"*Bonjour,* Annette," greeted Marie-Thérèse, finding her tongue. "Good day to you. Is there something wrong?"

"I need to talk to you. I need to talk to you NOW." Annette didn't even slow down. Still walking, she took Marie-Thérèse by one elbow and propelled her toward the washhouse.

It took Marie-Thérèse several steps before she realized that Annette was aiming the two of them directly for the washhouse door. She pulled her arm free and stopped to stare at her sister-in-law. "We're using the washhouse for an infirmary, now," she protested. "Why do you want to go into the infirmary? There are only two of *les moyennes* sick, now, and they're about well. Old Sister Ste. Madeleine is there to watch them. I'm not needed there."

"That's all the better. It'll be quiet. NOW," said Annette, pushing Marie-Thérèse inside the door. She panted a moment, catching her breath. "Tell me. What did you say to that man Cadillac?"

"Say?" At first, Marie-Thérèse was completely puzzled. "Why nothing at all. Except . . . oh dear!" she stopped, horrified.

"Well?" demanded Annette.

"Did I offend him at the ball? Oh, I hope I didn't! He didn't act offended, though I'm afraid he could have been. I did say one thing really awful. I asked him if being a privateer would get in the way

79

of watching the English as he does—watching them for King Louis, is what I meant. I felt terrible when I heard myself say it, because it sounded like I was calling him a spy. But he didn't act angry at all—he just laughed." Marie-Thérèse shook her head a little, remembering Monsieur Cadillac's expression. "I mean, he *really* laughed—right out loud. He acted as if he liked what I said."

Annette looked grim. "No, I don't think you made him angry. What else did you tell him? Did you say how wealthy we are? Did you tell him that your father put money away for you for your dowry?"

"No! Of course not! What is this about? Please tell me, please!" Marie-Thérèse was frantic. Until a few moments ago it had been a lovely day. Whenever she thought about the governor's ball, she had felt good. It was true that she'd been a little disappointed the night before, but when the morning came, all she could think of was what a good time she'd had, and how beautiful everything had been. Perhaps she'd only danced that one dance with Monsieur Cadillac, but then no one else had danced with him at all. And Al-soom-se had seen him watching her later on, after they'd danced. That meant he had liked her—or so she hoped. . . .

Annette was still talking. "Listen to me, Marie-Thérèse. Antoine de Lamothe Cadillac is at least ten years older than you are. He is a successful man. He does not need to call upon spinsters. There must be some reason that he has asked your brother Michel for permission to come and meet with you. Think! What did you tell him? He is a businessman, and he always needs money. Are you sure you didn't tell him about your dowry?"

"I didn't know I had a dowry," said Marie-Thérèse faintly. "I mean, not that I had one that was so big that anyone would care. Do I?"

"Yes you do," replied Annette with quiet emphasis. "I did not begrudge it to you when you were of marriageable age. Your father intended the money to attract the best possible match for you. I did not mind when Michel offered all of it and more to the Ursulines, if they would take you as one of them. You would have been settled for life. But you drove your suitors away with your impossible manners each time that they called. You have not married—and now you are almost too old to be married. You have told the good sisters that neither will you be a nun. I despair of you and what is to become of you, but it is time for the money to be put to good use. Michel and I have supported you ever since your father's death, and it looks as if we must support you for the rest of your life. I have told Michel your dowry should be ours. We will continue to provide a home for you, but we also will use the money to provide for our children when they come. You can help us with the children, and someday, perhaps, with the children's children. There are many such arrangements, and they are fair for everyone.

"But now, this morning, here comes the wildest privateer in *Nouvelle France,* hat in hand, asking to call on you—sounding like any of the boys from Lower Town. And he is eager to see you, of all people—you who have sent away all the young men in Québec. This much interest cannot happen in one dance at one ball. I ask you again: have you met with him before? He owns land in Port Royal. Did you meet him in Port Royal when your father was helping to repair the city walls?"

"No, of course not," Marie-Thérèse replied faintly. And then, louder, "No! How could I? When could I? Even if Papa knew Monsieur Cadillac, he would not have brought him home. Not in Port Royal. All the time we were there, Mama was far too sick to entertain guests."

It took Marie-Thérèse a long time to convince Annette that she had not spoken with Monsieur Cadillac anywhere but at the ball. Then it took even longer to remember and report every word she had said to him during the dance. At last Annette began to relax. But still she frowned at her sister-in-law.

"It seems you are innocent enough," she said. "Though I still can't see why Monsieur Cadillac should want to come to see you after the way you spoke to him—if you really said those things. Whatever got into you? . . . Never mind!" she added hastily, as Marie-Thérèse started to explain some more. "Not that any of it matters, really, as long as you have not embarrassed the family in some way." There was a smothered giggle off in the shadows of the wash house, and Marie-Thérèse suddenly remembered the two *moyennes* and their measles rashes.

Annette paid no attention to her small audience. She straightened her dress and flicked at it where she could see a spot of dust. Then she turned back to Marie-Thérèse. "You should know that Michel has not granted this Monsieur Cadillac permission to call on you personally until we understand better what it is he has in mind. You may be a joke, you know—with your talk of women exploring the wilderness. It's quite possible that the man is only seeking amusing tales to tell his friends. We will see, though. Michel has invited him to dine with us after mass this Sunday. Come home then, Marie-Thérèse. We will all talk with this Antoine Laumet de Lamothe Cadillac together," and Annette turned and swept out of the door of the washhouse as if she were making a grand exit from the governor's ballroom.

Marie-Thérèse turned apologetically to Sister Ste. Madeleine. "That is my sister-in-law," she said—hoping that explained things a little.

"She cares about her money, that one," replied Sister Ste. Madeleine, showing that she had heard everything and didn't need much explanation, "but I think she cares about you, too." Marie-Thérèse snorted.

Annette had talked so long that it was almost time for *les moyennes'* dancing class. Marie-Thérèse left the washhouse and walked slowly back toward the schoolroom. Sunday after mass was five whole days away.

Five days. That was enough time for Monsieur Cadillac to change his mind. But even if he did change his mind, she could know that at least for a time he thought about seeing her again. He must have talked to Michel that very morning—or maybe even last night, if Michel waited until morning to say anything to Annette. Both men had been at the Château St. Louis until late the night before with plenty of time to talk. Perhaps they hadn't gone to bed at all. She'd heard that smaller parties often broke off after a ball, and that some people played cards and entertained until dawn.

Marie-Thérèse stood still, looking blankly at the schoolroom door. She hardly knew how she'd gotten there. She was so busy thinking, she didn't remember walking that far. Her head spun. Monsieur Cadillac may have laughed last night, but he wasn't laughing at her any more. He liked her. He must like her. And if Antoine de Lamothe Cadillac liked her at all, it was for herself, not for her manners or lack of them.

❧   ❧   ❧

So it was that, on the following Sunday, Marie-Thérèse stood on the stoop outside Michel's front door. She felt far more nervous than she had been at the governor's ball. Her hands were wet and clammy, and she scrubbed at them with the handkerchief Anne had given her as she left the monastery grounds. "For luck," Anne said, as she pressed the gift into her friend's hands.

"I need luck. I need a miracle," Marie-Thérèse thought, and opened the door. The tall clock stood facing her, looking just as if nothing out of the ordinary was happening. Its dial read 1:00. It must have just struck the hour. She was on time—just barely. She could hear voices from the rooms at the back of the house. A man said something, and another laughed. She took a deep breath and hurried down the corridor toward the dining parlor.

The long banquet table was lined with faces. Antoine Laumet de Lamothe Cadillac was there, of course—the first person she saw—but so were Michel and Uncle François. Even her brother Jacques had joined them. The brothers were laughing merrily—apparently at something Monsieur Cadillac had just said. François must have heard the joke before, for he had pushed himself back from the table and sat waiting for the laughter to die down. Annette, at the head of the table, smiled with and at them all, like a queen amused by her court. Next to Annette was an empty chair, and Marie-Thérèse slid into it quickly, trying not to look up at the men.

"And now we are all here," cried Annette gaily. "We can eat this lovely meal that Brigitte has prepared for us!" She clapped her hands lightly, and the heavy-set *habitante* (farmer) woman who did the cooking appeared in the kitchen door. "Bring in the fish, Brigitte. I'm sure our guests are hungry."

The guests may have been hungry, but Marie-Thérèse was not. She choked on her fish, and when it was followed by roasted duckling, she made no attempt to eat the oily dish. She pulled most of the meat off the bones and pushed it around on her plate. At least it looked as if she had swallowed some of it. A glass of wine made her throat feel less dry. *"Pardon, Monsieur?"* she said, vaguely aware that Monsieur Cadillac had asked her a question.

"I asked you if you had ever told François, here, what your friend's brother had to say about his journey west."

Marie-Thérèse was surprised to see that both Uncle François and Michel were looking at her with real interest. "Do you mean about the trip to see the great falls?" Cadillac nodded.

Encouraged, Marie-Thérèse explained about the Iroquois

trails in the forest and the easy canoe trip that became harder as the waters moved faster. She described the rocks where Al-soom-se's brother had hidden. Annette's expression slowly changed from horror at the masculine subject matter of the conversation to amazement—as the men listened intently to Marie-Thérèse's tale.

"It's a rough *portage* at those falls . . . a long one, too," agreed Michel. "It's hard enough to carry hundreds of pounds of goods and the canoe besides, without having to carry them over that long a distance. But it's still the best way to reach the western lakes—or it would be if it weren't for the Iroquois threat."

"The Iroquois are there to stay—and the Algonquin," objected Cadillac. "They both more or less travel the river at will. The *portage* is long, but there's a good trail. The Iroquois use it especially because it runs all along the northern edge of their hunting grounds. And there's talk that Denonville is going to strengthen LaSalle's old fort above the falls. That and a decent treaty with the Iroquois should encourage our bold *coureurs de bois* to take the southern route again."

"I'd still rather not have some Iroquois warrior driving flaming splinters under my fingernails," interrupted Uncle François grimly.

Cadillac was undeterred. "I promise you," he pronounced, one finger tapping the table for emphasis, "when that fort is in place and the treaty signed, the best way to go west will be the easiest way, as well. And that way will be the one that Marie-Thérèse here has just described."

This was all too much for Annette. "It is time for Marie-Thérèse and me to leave you gentlemen to your tobacco and cognac," she smiled. "Come along, Marie-Thérèse," she said, patting her sister-in-law's shoulder. "This talk is not for us."

"But, Annette . . ." Marie-Thérèse began, and then stopped. Monsieur Cadillac closed one eye in an unmistakable wink. He grinned and jerked his head in the direction of Annette's departing back. It didn't feel like a dismissal. It was more like a conspiracy—a shared joke at Annette's squeamishness. Marie-Thérèse found herself smiling back. She rose, bowed slightly in farewell to Michel, Uncle François, and Monsieur Cadillac, and turned toward the hall.

Annette was waiting for her in the parlor, a strange look on her face. "You may have done it, little sister. You may have done it after all!" Annette chuckled in disbelief. "I almost think you could have brought in that awful beaver pelt and Monsieur Cadillac would not have cared . . . but are you sure? Are you sure you want a man like that?"

"I don't have him yet," replied Marie-Thérèse, suddenly liking her sister-in-law far better than she ever had before. Annette wasn't just spoiled and prissy. She really didn't know how wonderful the wilderness was, or how people could feel about seeing it for the first time. She didn't understand, and what she didn't understand she feared—for herself and for Marie-Thérèse. Old Sister Ste. Madeleine was right. Annette did care about her—at least some. "But yes, I'm sure," Marie-Thérèse finished, giving her surprised sister-in-law an impulsive hug.

❖ 12 ❖
Madame Cadillac

"**Y**ou've done it, Marie-Thérèse! You've done it! One dance and the man is in love with you!" Anne spun her friend around in a circle and then thumped her on the back so hard that Marie-Thérèse coughed.

"Easy, Anne! This ground is rough!" Marie-Thérèse staggered slightly and put out a hand to brace herself against an upright timber. The three were sweeping the hard floor of the monastery's makeshift chapel with stiff brooms made of bundled twigs. When the packed dirt had been a stable floor, the feet of horses and convent workers tamped the soil down until it seemed almost as hard as marble—but it was a hardness that didn't last. Now, as nuns and students walked to and fro in the aisleways, the very top layer of dust-fine earth worked loose. It lay there in small, dusty heaps—reminding them that the chapel was, after all, only a barn. Each day someone had to sweep out the worst of it. This afternoon it filled the air in yellow-brown clouds as Marie-Thérèse, Anne, and Al-soom-se swept their way toward the wide entrance to the stable. Wind blew in toward them, taking part of each broom stroke and blowing the dirt back whence it had come. "Tell me again why we volunteered to do this job, will you?" grunted Marie-Thérèse.

"Because it was either do some kind of productive work here or spend the afternoon being polite to Madame Denonville," replied Anne. "I swear that she thinks I have become her personal musician—and since I can't go to the Château alone, either all of us go, or all of us stay. This was the only way I could think to stay here. I really don't like playing the harpsichord for other people."

"Mmmm-hmmm," Marie-Thérèse nodded her understanding. She dug harder at a dried lump in the ground that looked more like something that had come out of a stall than like plain dirt. "I don't know, Anne, Al . . . I think Monsieur Cadillac likes me well enough, but so far he treats me much the same way he treats my brothers," Marie-Thérèse finished a little uncomfortably.

"Anne's right, though," Al-soom-se's voice was firm. "Antoine de Lamothe Cadillac does not have time to pay casual visits to young ladies. He has seen you and he likes what he sees. Uncle Pierre says that it won't be long before Monsieur Cadillac will be sent west to explore trade routes beyond the land of the Huron. He will want to marry before he leaves. He may not love you exactly—at least not yet—but I think he will not look for anyone else to be his wife."

"There. You see?" Anne said, as if Al-soom-se had offered proof. "He has to travel west. He's even asked you for information about the southern route. I'll bet he would go that way if the Iroquois were not so hostile. That proves that he thinks you are perfect to be his wife."

"It 'proves' nothing at all, Anne, and you know it." Marie-Therese said glumly. "You should have heard Mother Mary of the Angels this morning. She certainly didn't talk about marriage— at least not much."

Al-soom-se looked up sharply. "I saw your brother Michel go in to see Mother Superior today. It was very early—maybe an hour after mass. Did Mother Mary talk to you after that?"

"It was actually pretty late, almost time to eat dinner. I was sitting with *les petites,* listening to them recite their sums, and she came into the schoolroom and took me right out of the class. She walked me all the way to the convent before she started to talk. You know how she sometimes looks at you before saying anything? Well, today she just stared and stared at me. Finally she said, 'Are you certain in your heart that you do not wish to serve God as a nun?' As if she didn't know the answer to that after that scene I made! I said that yes, I was certain, and then she asked me if I was equally sure I was 'ready' to be a wife. I told her I could do household accounts, and she looked so sad, it really bothered me! I tried to get her to tell me what she was talking about, and she suddenly stopped looking sad, and she just grinned at me. 'I'm checking on one of my charges, that is all!' she said—and that was the only thing that I could get out of her."

"Oh, don't you see?" cried Al-soom-se. "Your brother has withdrawn his offer to the monastery. He's no longer going to pay them to make you a nun. Mother Mary just wants to be sure you are doing what you want to do with your life."

"But then why in the world did she look so sad when I told her I could do household accounts?" Marie-Thérèse wondered.

"Maybe because she was thinking that, for you, marriage has to be much more than running a household. She hopes you know that about yourself. You know it's true. The richest holdings in the world would bore you if you had to stay there and run them all the time. She knows us all better than we think," answered Anne.

Thunder rumbled in the distance. Al-soom-se sniffed the air. It smelled and felt damp, and the dampness was mixed with the sharp scent that warns of heavy weather. "What I think is that we had better hurry and finish our sweeping before it rains," she said. "If we have dust on our skirts and get caught in the storm, we'll look as if we'd been rolling in the mud. But I promise you, Marie-Thérèse. The next time you are called home, it will be to hear a proposal of marriage."

"And is that how it happened, Madame?" small René asked the old lady. He knew that he shouldn't have interrupted her, but this part of the story always bored him a little. "Is that how you were married?"

Madame Cadillac caught her breath and reached for the tea that someone had placed near her. She sipped at it slowly and did not answer right away. *Mon Dieu!* But she had been talking for a long time. The sun was dropping toward the Castelsarrasin rooftops. One or two of the smaller ones in her audience had fallen asleep, but the rest of the children sat at careful attention, not wanting to miss a word. She felt a small hand tug at her skirt and looked down. "Yes, René, that's how it happened—or almost. The next afternoon they asked me to go home for a 'meeting.' Antoine met me, all right! Right there at the doorway of my brother's house. We went straight into the parlor and planned our wedding and marriage. I don't believe he ever actually asked me to marry him. He simply gave me no chance to say that I would not!"

She stopped speaking and looked across the courtyard, not really seeing anything except Antoine—just as if he was standing before her. All these years later, she still could see the twinkle in his eyes. "Call me Antoine," he had demanded as soon as they sat down. They were facing each other across the front room, almost as they had done at their first meeting. "Call me Antoine, and I will call you Thérèse. I am leaving for Port Royal in three weeks' time. You need to gather your things and prepare for the wedding. You can manage to be ready before the third week of June, can't you?" She could hear his voice as clearly as if he were speaking today.

"Madame!" said René, tugging harder at her skirt.

"Yes, René." Madame Cadillac broke out of her daydream. "I went home, I met with Antoine, and we planned our wedding. He hadn't even left us enough time to have the banns properly posted. In those days, just as now, the church expected couples to announce their weddings three times, one time each week for the three weeks before they were wed. That way, if anyone felt they should not be married, the wedding could be stopped in time. But there was no stopping Antoine!" She laughed in remembered delight, sounding not much older than René himself. "Or me, either. I was almost seventeen years old. I knew I'd not get another offer of marriage—at least not another good one, as old as I was. And I did so want to marry Antoine. We posted our banns on June 22 and again on June 24, got special permission from the Bishop of Québec so that we didn't need to do it a third time, and were married on June 25, 1687. And then we went to Port Royal to live."

"That's where you got captured by pirates, isn't it?" said René with satisfaction. "That was in Port Royal."

"Yes, René, that was in Port Royal—but was not for a while, yet. That wasn't until almost exactly three years later, in 1690. I had two children by then. Small Joseph had been born just after the new year. He was just beginning to try to crawl. His big sister Judith was a great girl of eighteen months. Poor Judith."

"Why 'poor Judith,' Madame? You never told us there was anything bad about her," said René anxiously.

"There was nothing bad about Judith. She was my angel," smiled Madame Cadillac. She looked around her. There was still time. It would be light for hours, yet. She took a last swallow of tea and went on with her story.

❖   ❖   ❖

"May, again," remarked Marie-Thérèse to herself, watching her daughter as she pulled herself across the floor by her elbows. Judith had taken to copying her baby brother. Joseph was just beginning to crawl, and so now Judith must pretend to crawl too. Copying was something that Judith did very well. It had taken Marie-Thérèse a long time to face the fact that Judith probably would not be able to do very many things equally well. In the long months before Judith was born, yet another measles epidemic had swept through New France. This time, Marie-Thérèse had caught the disease. She wasn't much sickened by it, she remembered. She had the rash, and a bit of fever, her eyes burned and she was very, very tired, but that was all. She hadn't understood then why the other women in Port Royal were so worried about her. It was Al-soom-se, there for a visit, who explained.

"Sometimes if a woman has measles before a baby is born, the baby gets the disease. And then that baby, when it grows up, is not like other babies. Sometimes it does not think clearly. Sometimes it is blind. Sometimes it cannot hear."

Judith could not hear. At first no one noticed. The baby was so good, and slept so well, and smiled so much. And she copied everything. If you made a face at Judith, she made it back. If you held your hand just so, Judith would hold her hand the same way. But when you spoke—when you spoke, Judith just moved her mouth—and then giggled and laughed as if she'd done something very special. Now she scootched her way across the board floor and caught at her mother's feet and laughed her best gurgly laugh.

"All right," laughed Marie-Thérèse in her turn. She pulled her daughter to her feet. "Come. Let us see if your brother is awake."

Much had changed in Marie-Thérèse's world since her marriage to Antoine. France and England always were uneasy friends. Now, with King William on the throne in England, the two countries were at war in earnest. Marie-Thérèse knew that this had something to do with the fact that the old English king, James II, hadn't minded that France was a Catholic nation. But King William was just the opposite. He distrusted the French partly because they *were* Catholic, and he was quick to fight against them when war broke out in Europe. "It seems so silly," Marie-Thérèse remarked to Antoine, "to hate people because they don't agree with your religion. If we felt like that, we should have to kill every Abenaki and Iroquois who didn't go to the monastery school. We'd never stop hating and killing, and there'd be no time to make New France into a nation." Her fingers flew over her knitting. When she was annoyed, she knitted faster, and now she knitted very fast indeed.

"King William owes his throne to the fact that he is protestant," Antoine replied. "That made choosing sides in this war easy for him. And now he and his English soldiers will see to it that the Iroquois do their raiding where it will hurt us the most. Of course, the Iroquois did your friend a favor."

Marie-Thérèse looked up frowning. "Whatever do you mean?"

"They drove Denonville back home to France, of course—and now your Anne will never have to play the harpsichord for Madame Denonville again!" Antoine ducked his head just in time to miss the ball of yarn that Marie-Thérèse threw at him.

In the first two years of their marriage, Antoine and Marie-Thérèse had far too few chances for conversation. They were apart almost more than they were together. This May he was at Fort de Buade—finally making the long-planned trip to the great waters. Marie-Thérèse thought happily about how excited he'd been when he knew of the assignment. He'd paced up and down in their small front room, talking about what led to his good fortune.

"I spent a year watching the British where they've settled the lands to our south. You know that I traveled all the way from New England through New York and as far south as the Carolinas. I reported to King Louis, telling him everything that I saw—fortifications, armaments, everything. To count the people, I even checked to see how many churches had been built. This year I've watched the English from the sea, instead of the land. I've had to. They are working their way toward us right here in Acadia—going as far east as they can go in New France. And then, of course, there was that storm at sea. You know, I think that the best thing that could have happened to me was that storm." He stopped walking and looked at Marie-Thérèse. "If I hadn't been blown out to sea, I'd not have had to travel all the way to France to make a landfall. And if it had not taken so long for the king to send me home again, our good Governor Frontenac would not have felt sorry for me that I was kept so long from Port Royal and you." He took both Marie-Thérèse's hands in his. "Now, because he feels sorry, he has given me the chance to explore to the west."

"Let me understand this," replied Marie-Thérèse wryly. "Governor Frontenac feels sorry because you have been kept from me, and so to reward you he sends you away again?"

Antoine had the grace to look a little sheepish. He dropped

her hands. "You'll be all right. You've Gaspard and the other two Abenaki to help you on the land. And I promise: this time, when I return, we'll talk about ways to take you back west with me." Marie-Thérèse nodded. She'd heard Antoine say that before.

Yet Antoine was right. She had grown to depend a great deal on the teen-aged Abenaki Gaspard, and Gaspard, in turn, was fiercely loyal to her and to the children. He owed his life to Antoine, who had ransomed him from an Iroquois war party. Gaspard would like to have fought and brought many Iroquois scalps to Monsieur Cadillac to show his appreciation. But Monsieur Cadillac asked only that Madame Cadillac be guarded well. In his own village, Gaspard could have been laughed at for working the earth and tending cattle. It was mostly women's work. But this woman was Monsieur Cadillac's woman. If he worked with her, he was there to guard her, and so Gaspard learned to do women's work in the *canadienne* way. He helped Marie-Thérèse teach the other Abenaki guards to use a plow and care for cattle. They learned quickly, possibly because the two had been to schools taught by the "black-robes." They knew even more than Gaspard that, among the *Canadiens,* such work was honorable.

With three pairs of eager hands to help her, it was almost easy for Marie-Thérèse to run the farm. She had only to keep up the small house and oversee the work done in the nearby fields. And take care of the children, of course! Marie-Thérèse leaned forward quickly to pull small Joseph away from the hearth. She had not been quite quick enough. His shirt front was covered with ashes. She scrubbed at it with her hand.

"Come." She beckoned to Judith as she said the word. "It's too nice a day to be indoors anyway. You and your brother can sit in the garden for a while."

⚜ 13 ⚜
A War, an Escape, and a Pirate

This is not such a bad arrangement, Marie-Thérèse thought contentedly, as she watched her children playing in the sunshine behind the house. It was easy to feel happy. The earliest plantings were beginning to show above the neat rows tilled in the soil. The new calf kicked up its heels in the cow pen. The morning's baking was done and the good smell of bread still hung in the air.

Marie-Thérèse leaned back against the wall of her house and smiled up at the sun. Her fingers found a loose spot in the chinking between the logs, and she played with it until it came loose. "Drat!" she thought. She shoved the piece of chinking back between the logs and made a mental note to ask Gaspard to fix it properly. She liked her little house, with its vertical logs facing the world like a miniature stockade. She gave one log a pat. The English were so strange. She'd heard they built all their cabins of logs piled on top of one another. It took so much more time to build that way, and took so many more logs. The log home that Antoine had commissioned for her was temporary, but cozy. Soon they would move their furnishings into a timber and masonry home as fine as any in Québec. She looked to her left. There on a little rise in the land, she could see the frame going up for the new house. But her little house was solid and comfortable and filled with things to make living easy. It would do nicely until Antoine came home again.

"Madame! Madame!" There was a commotion at the front door.

"Around back, Gaspard," she called.

Gaspard appeared around the corner of the house, breathing

heavily. He had been running, and it took him a moment before he was able to speak. "Madame, you must take the babies and as much food and clothing and money as you can. The British come up the river. People say seven warships, full of soldiers." He paused and swallowed. "They reach Port Royal tomorrow morning. Maybe sooner. We must hide you. If English soldiers find Monsieur Cadillac's family here alone. . . ." He didn't finish. "Hurry. We go into the woods."

"What about the others?" Marie-Thérèse looked about for the other two young Abenaki men.

"They have gone already, Madame. Please?" and Gaspard gestured toward the house.

Marie-Thérèse didn't hesitate further. She reached for little Joseph and felt his napkin. It was dry. "Good," she thought. "That's one thing I don't have to do just now." She strapped him quickly onto the cradle-board Al-soom-se had given her when Judith was born. Cradle-boards were a wonderful way to carry babies and still have your hands free. She could never understand why more *canadienne* mothers didn't adopt the Abenaki way. She looked around the farmyard. Two large empty grain sacks lay against the lean-to behind the house. They were dusty and stiff, but they were perfect for her purpose. She ducked back outside and grabbed the sacks and carried them up to the sleeping loft. Quickly, she stuffed one with clothing—shawls for herself and Judith, napkins for the baby. There was room for only one blanket. Well, it was May. Perhaps the night would not be too cold. Hurrying back down the narrow steps, she started on the other bag. Into it she tossed a pouch that held the household money and three or four pieces of her jewelry. Then she paused. Where were the ruby earrings Antoine had brought from France? She found them at the back of a drawer where she'd pushed them to keep them safe from exploring baby fingers. Fumbling, she fastened them in her ears. There was a small scuffling next to her. Judith was bobbing and weaving on fat, unsteady legs.

"No, sweetheart, it's not to be a party." Marie-Thérèse wasn't sure how much Judith could understand, so she always spoke as if the child followed every word. "But we are going to have an adventure." She pushed the toddler before her gently. They came into the kitchen together, just as Gaspard reappeared in the doorway.

"We leave now, Madame," he said. With one arm, he swept

Judith up onto his shoulders, where she sat giggling happily. He reached for the sacks Marie-Thérèse was dragging. She indicated the one full of clothing and kept hold of the other.

"Just a moment more," she said. In the pantry, the day's baking of bread stood ready. That went into the sack she had kept, along with a bag of meal. Dried apples! Yes, they would boil into a sauce for Judith, presuming there could be a fire. She took the apples and a pot of honey. A small iron pot came next. At the last she grabbed her large carving knife. "I hope I need it only for food," she thought grimly. "I'm ready now," she said aloud.

All looked peaceful enough as they set out, walking deeper and deeper into the forest. The plan was to walk well away from the Port Royal habitation and then turn back toward the water—not just because the fresh streams flowing into the river would provide drinking water, but because the river could be a source of news. Marie-Thérèse was exhausted, and, by the time they halted in a clearing, Joseph—fretful on his cradle-board—seemed to weigh as much as the new calf they'd left behind in its pen. This would be no permanent camp. They must always be ready to move ahead of discovery, but at least for the moment they could rest.

❖   ❖   ❖

Under any other circumstances, the next three weeks would have been among the happiest in Marie-Thérèse's life. The spring days were lovely. The weather stayed warm and sunny. The forest was alive with the sound of birds. One day, Judith turned up missing. Searching frantically, Marie-Thérèse found her curled up next to a fawn—two babies sleeping together in a nest of tall grasses. "The sisters would say it was like the Garden of Eden," Marie-Thérèse thought to herself.

Hunting was good, and, with no sign of other human beings anywhere, Marie-Thérèse could build a small cooking fire. But the days stretched into weeks. The time came that the last apple was soaked and pounded into a gruel for the babies. The forest that seemed so friendly and welcoming began to feel like a giant, green sea—washing Marie-Thérèse and her little ones away from all she knew.

"When can we leave here safely, do you think?" she asked Gaspard. She was deftly stripping the skin from a squirrel. "Baked in mud with his jacket on," she explained to wide-eyed Judith. "That way he stays nice and juicy for you to eat."

Gaspard squatted down by the small fire. "I went to Port Royal," he replied, "on my last hunt for food. I learned much. These English not from over the water. They come from a place called 'Mass-a-chu-setts.' Mass-a-chu-setts chief, William Phips, does not love the *canadien*. He plans to attack and capture Montreal. This because Governor Frontenac attacks English settlements."

Marie-Thérèse nodded. She could understand Phips's reasoning. Count Frontenac, named governor after Denonville was recalled to France, treated all English as enemies of both old and New France. There had been many terrible raids on English farms and villages in New England.

Gaspard continued to speak. "Meneval"—he almost spat the word—"Meneval is not a fit governor for Port Royal. He gives all Port Royal to this Phips. He does not fight at all. He met Phips the first morning that ships come. Meneval gives Phips money, and they are as friends. Phips told soldiers not to burn Port Royal, but soldiers act like soldiers. Much damage was done. Soldiers learned Monsieur Cadillac live in Port Royal. They very angry that he was not there to pay for spying on English. They call him eyes for men who burn English settlements. They say he cost many English lives." Marie-Thérèse nodded again. She had never fooled herself about the reasons that Antoine "watched" the English for King Louis.

"Madame," Gaspard's sober Abenaki face grew even bleaker. "Madame, they burned everything on the farm. I saw. They killed the calf—everything. But now today Phips is gone. He took ships and went away to Montreal. Some English stay in Port Royal, but it is safe now to go to the river. There are French ships in the river."

Marie-Thérèse bit her lip and stared at the squirrel meat in her hands. She tossed it in the pot and straightened up. "Then let us eat and go. The sooner we find the French, the sooner we can get word to Antoine that the babies and I are all right."

"I did that already, Madame," replied Gaspard. "I told the Abenaki. Monsieur Cadillac will hear. I also sent word to Madame Cadillac's brothers in Québec. You go there to live until Monsieur Cadillac comes. When you and babies are with brothers, I go myself to Monsieur Cadillac. If he does not come back with me, he will tell me what to do."

Marie-Thérèse smiled for the first time since Gaspard had begun his story. She threw her arms around his neck and hugged him—hard—and then laughed out loud to see the look on his face. "You are truly wonderful, *mon ami,* my friend! Antoine could have left his family in no better hands."

The little group made its careful way to the shores of the river, Judith, as before, riding on Gaspard's shoulders. She sucked and chewed happily at a hard biscuit brought from Port Royal. "Better and better," Marie-Thérèse marveled when she saw it. "Her new teeth bother her so."

Gaspard shrugged, stepping back lest he be hugged again. "This is nothing, Madame. Many biscuits in Port Royal. English bring them in ships and trade for soft bread."

Afterwards, Marie-Thérèse could not decide whether they were lucky or unfortunate that the brig *Amitié* picked that day to travel upriver to Montreal. Fresh from France and unaware they were sailing past lands now held by the English, her sailors waved gaily at the small party on the shore. It took some time to get the crew to understand, but finally the *Amitié* put down a small boat. Even then the sailors were somewhat taken aback when Marie-Thérèse, Gaspard, and the children waded out to meet them and scrambled into the boat before it put ashore.

Brought before the *Amitié*'s captain, Marie-Thérèse explained. The captain listened carefully. He was grateful for the news about Phips and his fleet, if more than a little alarmed by it. But Marie-Thérèse presented him with a problem. He could not very well leave a Frenchwoman and two infants on the shore with only a teen-aged Abenaki for chaperone and protection. Neither could he go into battle with a woman and children aboard, and he couldn't be sure that Phips had left no ship behind to patrol the river. He thought and thought and worried and worried. Finally, since the *Amitié* already had passed Port Royal without incident, he decided that the water, at least, was still French. Phips's raiding party may have been lucky at Port Royal, but the captain doubted they'd be successful against a larger city. The *Amitié* had a full load to deliver to Montreal, and so he would merely deliver his passengers there at the same time.

The captain gave orders that his new passengers be fed from the officers' mess, where they would find the best food remaining on a ship that had just crossed the Atlantic Ocean. He moved himself into his lieutenant's cabin, gave over his own to Marie-Thérèse and the children, and told his officers to make room for Gaspard in their quarters. He posted a lookout at the masthead and went to sleep, content that he had done his duty.

The captain's rest lasted less time than it took Marie to wash out small Joseph's napkins. She was hanging them in the ship's rigging to dry—or trying to do so, over the protests of a young boy who appeared to be one of the ship's officers—when she heard a single loud "BOOM!" "Not cannon. It can't be cannon—not out here in the middle of nowhere," she remarked to Judith. To keep her from falling overboard, the little girl was tied to her mother's waist with a strip of blanket. Joseph slept contentedly on the cradle-board.

"Get below, Madame! Go below now!!" the boy officer's shout answered her question. He pushed her toward a hatchway. Shoved along by brute force, Marie-Thérèse managed to turn her head back toward the direction of the sound. She could just see another ship, smaller than the French brig, nosing its way around a bend in the river. It was low to the water and narrower than the brig, and it had only two masts.

"A *corsaire,*" Marie-Thérèse thought, as she hurried toward the captain's cabin. She had seen the fast vessels in the harbor near Lower Town. They were used by privateers to overtake and capture merchant ships—but most of them were French. Why would a French privateer stop a French brig? "Because he's a pirate, not a legal privateer," she answered herself furiously. "That's funny. I'm not afraid; I'm just plain mad. Talk about 'out of the frying pan and into the fire!' Well, we'd best be ready for anything." She slammed her things together. Now that their food was eaten, all their belongings fitted into one large sack.

She was packed and standing with Joseph on her back and Judith cradled on one hip when the French captain opened the door to the cabin.

"Madame," he began, bowing courteously, "I regret to tell you that we have been detained by a Spanish privateer—a *corsaire*—the name we give to both him and his ship. We have cannon, but we are sailing upstream. He has only to put about and sail past us, and his guns can fire into us at will. We are carrying much gunpowder for the fort at Montreal. We cannot risk exploding—not with you and Monsieur Cadillac's children aboard. We have surrendered."

98

One word of the captain's formal little speech was a distinct surprise. "A Spaniard? So close to Québec?" Marie-Thérèse wondered aloud.

An hour later, standing as before, this time ducking her head because the low roof of the corsaire's cabin prevented her standing upright, she asked her question again in a sharper tone of voice. "What is a Spaniard doing this far north? And how dare you fire upon one of King Louis's ships?" she demanded of the small dark man seated before her.

"*Mademoiselle,* many pardons for my inconveniencing of you." The Spanish captain's French was accented, but it was understandable.

"Madame!" snapped Marie-Thérèse. "I am *Madame* Lamothe Cadillac, and I am a grand-niece of the Duc de Lauzon. You will stand and address me as a gentleman should." Her ruby earrings caught the sunlight coming through the cabin window and glowed. They danced with the force of her words.

The captain did not rise from his chair, but he made a gesture as if he were bowing. "My mistaking. Madame, then. And who is this 'Ca-dil-lac?' A wealthy man, no?" He glanced at her earrings. "Wealthy, to have a wife who gives herself such airs and wears such jewels even when she hides in the woods?"

Too late, Marie-Thérèse realized her error. The *Amitié's* captain must have tried to protect her by describing her as a refugee without telling the Spaniard exactly who she was. If she had been an ordinary citizen of Port Royal, the pirate might have set her ashore as an inconvenience—something he did not wish to have get in his way. But now he knew her value, and he was thinking of the money she might bring—enough money to make inconvenience worth while. Marie-Thérèse and the children would be held for ransom. "Well, at least we'll eat," she thought grimly.

"What about my servant?" she asked, ignoring the captain's question. If this pirate wanted her to stay valuable, he'd have to treat her—and those with whom she traveled—well. She'd have to see that he understood that. Even in the monastery she had heard stories of prisoners of the Iroquois who were tortured publicly so that people would be quicker to pay to free them from their captors. She had to make sure the Spaniard knew that torturing Antoine Cadillac's woman would cost the *corsaire* money, not increase her ransom value. With luck, perhaps she could extend that slim protection to Gaspard.

The captain was speaking again. "Where is your servant?" he echoed. "Alas, my men explain to him that he should be a sailor and not care for infants. He was not brave enough to be a sailor. He jumped into the water, Madame. We have not seen him since. He is a devil. If he did not drown, he has run away to hide in the woods with the rest of his kind. But we will take care of you now, Madame." The pirate actually was smiling—as if he expected Marie-Thérèse to smile back in gratitude.

Marie-Thérèse thought furiously. Gaspard would make his way to Cadillac and tell him what had happened. He probably also would get word to Michel. Michel would have to be the one to ransom her. "Annette will love that," she muttered to herself.

"Pardon?" the captain asked.

"Nothing for Spanish ears, *Capitán.*" Marie-Thérèse gave the Spanish title a slightly mocking sound. Yes, Michel would have to ransom her, but she actually might be back in Québec quicker this way than if she had remained aboard the brig all the way to Montreal. Yes. This actually was better—except for the money Michel would have to pay. She smiled finally, deliberately looking at the Spaniard in the submissive way she had been taught to look at her partners in a dance. "I ask your pardon in turn, Monsieur," she said—hoping she sounded charming. "You will understand when I say that I did not expect to need rescue twice in one day. The brig which you captured had just rescued me from the English. But—oh dear—those English must be your allies." Her dismay was partly put on and partly real as she realized that—if the Spanish were working with the English—she might find herself ransomed to someone like William Phips. But this Spanish captain knew nothing of the English desire for personal revenge on Antoine de Lamothe Cadillac.

The little *corsaire* rose from behind his desk. "The English fight the French, Madame. The Spanish fight the French. All of Europe fights each other in this war. The Spanish government likes best when I capture French ships. But I and my men, Madame, we capture English ships, too. And we have killed English sailors. Certainly we would kill Englishmen to capture so valuable a person as you yourself." He offered his arm and, after a moment, Marie-Thérèse rested her hand on it. "But you are tired now. We must settle you in my lieutenant's cabin, I think." Before Marie-Thérèse could protest, he added, "The cannon that are in my cabin stay cleared for action. We remain always ready to fight. Mine is a larger cabin, but is not a place for ladies to sleep." They reached the door. "Now tell me, Madame. Where do we find this Cadillac of yours?"

Marie-Thérèse ducked still lower to keep her head and Joseph's from hitting the door frame. Once in the companionway, she turned and faced the *corsaire* and a sentry that was posted outside the cabin door. "Did he think I was dangerous enough that he needed an armed guard?" Marie-Thérèse frowned to herself.

Aloud, she said, "My husband is far away and cannot ransom me, Monsieur. But I will tell you how to reach my brothers in Québec. They will pay you well, if I tell them you have treated me kindly—as I'm sure that you will," she finished with emphasis.

❖ 14 ❖

Holding the Fort

"I can't believe we're still doing laundry!" Anne laughed as she set the basket of clean clothes on the table before her and began pulling out items to fold. The sun was warm on her back. It warmed the basket, too, and from it rose the good smell of fabric dried in fresh air.

"I know," Marie-Thérèse was laughing, too. "Every time I do anything like this, I expect Sister Cécile to walk out that door. Instead, it's more likely to be one of the children."

Marie-Thérèse and Anne were indeed doing laundry again— only this time, instead of wading through a sea of bed linens at the monastery, they were in Québec, working in the sunny back garden of the house Antoine had found for his growing family.

Anne paused in her folding. "Isn't it strange the way you never think of time passing while you are doing something, and then you wake up one day and whole years have gone by?"

"It's even stranger when you measure time by the quantity of dirty clothes you've seen! At least it isn't a punishment this time," said Marie-Thérèse. "You know what? If Sister Cécile really were here, she'd have all the children somehow helping, even little Jacques." She nodded toward the cradle-board hanging on the shady side of the house.

"I dare say Jacques makes his contribution to the laundry— although in the wrong direction." Anne walked over to stare nose-to-nose at the sleeping baby. "He's a cute one, though." She touched his cheek. Jacques screwed his face up into a series of expressions, one of which might have been a smile. "Are the fine ladies of the city still shocked at the way your little ones look like

Abenaki babies? I envy you, though. Alphonse hasn't been home enough for us to start a family," for Anne had married Alphonse de Tonty, a dashing *voyageur* who served often as Antoine's second in command. "How do you manage, Marie-Thérèse? Four? Five children? How old are they all now? I thought you had a *habitante* woman helping out. Shouldn't she be here?"

"Claudette is a gem, and I couldn't keep this house without her." Marie-Thérèse answered the last question first. "Unfortunately, her husband agrees with me—at least about not being able to get things done without her. She's at her own place all this week, helping with the spring planting. Jacques, as you very well know, is Cadillac number five. But ages? Let me think . . .

"It's 1695, and Judith was born early in 1689. That makes her six-going-on-seven. So Joseph is five, Antoine three, Madeleine two, and you," she turned to Jacques, whose eyes were open now. "You sir, are five months old today. If we were back in Port Royal, we would have our own little celebration, but in Québec, *Tante* Annette rules. Tonight we must clean up and go visit her." The baby burbled happily and turned his head to look beyond his mother's shoulder where a swallowtail butterfly hovered and danced.

There was something in Marie-Thérèse's voice that caught Anne's attention. "Do you miss Port Royal and the farm terribly?" she asked quietly.

"There are days that I do," Marie-Thérèse replied honestly. "And I feel terrible when I do. But we've really been back and forth enough these last couple of years that I can't miss it that much. When Antoine isn't home, it's still safer to stay in the city. And, for the most part, I'm far too busy to think much about it." As if to make her point, two small forms shot from the back door of the house.

"You did, you did, you did!" accused the louder of the two voices. The answering voice was higher, but almost as loud. "Did not!" And then both voices jumbled together. "Did too! Did NOT! Did first!"

Joseph got to Marie-Thérèse a step ahead of his brother. "Mama! Mama! Make Antoine stop pinching me!"

With the ease that goes with frequent practice, Marie-Thérèse caught one son in each hand and held them both at arms' length. "Well?" she asked, looking at the smaller of the two figures.

Petit Antoine's lower lip stuck out stubbornly. "Pinched first," he said accusingly, pointing to his brother.

"Joseph, did you. . . ?" Marie-Thérèse took a firmer grip on her elder son. Joseph squirmed.

"Well, maybe just a little."

"Where are your sisters? Did you pinch them?"

"No!" Joseph was indignant. "I only pinched Antoine—but that was because he wouldn't give me my top. And he pinched me, too. Hard!" Rather belatedly, Joseph remembered his original complaint.

"Here come the girls now," remarked Anne. There in the doorway stood Judith, glaring disapprovingly at her brothers. She looked tall and regal next to her pudgy baby sister. Now she made a pushing motion, and Madeleine, the toddler, sat down obediently. Judith approached Marie-Thérèse, making pinching gestures with her hands. She pointed to Joseph, then to Antoine.

"Yes, *chérie,* I know." Marie-Thérèse turned the boys loose with a little swat and pushed her hair back with one hand. "I wish they could all be as good as you are." Judith still stood before her, unsure that her mother had understood. Marie-Thérèse bent down to Judith's level. Pinch, pinch, went Marie-Thérèse's hands. Then, slap, slap. She spanked an invisible figure and pointed to the boys. Judith beamed and nodded. Then, duty done, she went back to the doorway, tugged Madeleine to her feet, and the two were gone again.

"She's amazing," smiled Anne.

"Yes, isn't she? She's such good help with Madeleine, and Madeleine adores her. Some days she's more help than Claudette, I think. Without her, with this crowd coming and going all the time, I'd feel like Madeleine de Verchères."

Anne looked blank.

"You don't know about Madeleine de Verchères?" Marie-Thérèse asked.

Anne shook her head.

"I don't see how you could have missed hearing about it," Marie-Thérèse frowned. "Everybody talked about it when it happened. That's even how my Madeleine got her name. I mean, we named her Madeleine after Madeleine de Verchères.

"It was almost three years ago—in the fall of 1692. Madeleine de Verchères was fourteen years old. Her father ran—and runs—

Fort Verchères. It's more a trading post than a fort, really, but it has a blockhouse that connects to it with a walkway, and a number of cannon. You're sure you haven't heard this?" Anne shook her head.

"Madeleine's father had been called to Québec, her mother was visiting in Montreal, and Madeleine was home alone, or nearly so. This was in October—October 22. Harvest time. Everybody was working out in the fields except for two soldiers, her two little brothers, a bunch of women and children, an old man who was nearly eighty, and her hired man. Anyway, Madeleine and the hired man were down by the river doing laundry. . . ."

Anne looked up.

"Yes, laundry, again!" grinned Marie-Thérèse. "We must be the cleanest nation in the New World! So Madeleine was doing laundry, and suddenly she and Laviolette (that's the hired man) heard gunfire coming from the direction of the fields. He yelled at her to run, and she turned and saw about fifty Iroquois running toward them. They were really close—maybe fifty or sixty feet away from her. She ran as fast as she could, and when they realized they couldn't catch her, the Iroquois started shooting. She could hear the bullets go past her head. She shouted 'To arms!' at the fort, hoping somebody would come rescue her. Nothing happened. When she finally got up to the gate, her way was blocked by a couple of women whose husbands had just been killed. The women were in pretty bad shape, but she somehow got them ahead of her and pushed them and Laviolette into the fort and shut the gate behind them all. Then she ran around ordering the people who were there inside the fort to set up the palisades where they had been taken down for ventilation. Once she was sure the Iroquois were locked out, she went hunting for the soldiers. She found them hiding in the blockhouse where all the gunpowder and ammunition was stored. No wonder they hadn't come to rescue her! One of the soldiers was holding a lighted match. She asked him what he thought he was doing, and he told her he was going to blow the place up and kill them all so that the Iroquois couldn't get them and torture them. Madeleine yelled at him for being a coward and ran him out of the place.

"After her look at the soldiers, she figured the only people she could count on were her brothers. They were pretty little—aged ten and twelve—but they could shoot. That was more than Laviolette had ever done. He'd never fired a gun in his life.

MADELEINE DES VERCHÈRES. In this chapter, Marie-Thérèse tells Anne the exciting story of Madeleine des Verchères. Here, Madeleine and her hired man, Laviolette, have just reached the gates of Fort Verchères. Madeleine hasn't taken charge of the fort yet, but she's about to realize that the soldiers are hiding and that it is up to her to save everyone from the attack. Notice that, for a change, no one is wearing court fashions. These people are dressed in clothing that is suitable for the hard work they do every day. (C. W. Jefferys, *The Iroquois Attack of Fort Verchères, 1692. Madeleine Closes the Gate,* National Archives of Canada, C-010687. Reproduced with permission of the C. W. Jefferys Estate, Toronto, Ontario, Canada.)

Anyway, Madeleine took off her bonnet and put on a hat so that she'd look more like a man if the Iroquois saw her. Then, with her brothers, she ran around shooting at the Iroquois from the loopholes in the fort. It was enough to scare the Iroquois into thinking the fort was full of soldiers, and the warriors fell back to finish killing the people who were still in the fields.

"The Iroquois were almost easier to deal with than the women and children. The women were making such a racket screaming and crying that Madeleine was afraid the Iroquois would guess there were no men there to guard them. Somehow she made them all shut up. I don't know how. Maybe she threatened to shoot them, too. Once she got everybody quiet, she started firing cannon to scare the Iroquois. She hoped the shots would also serve to warn any soldiers in the area that the fort was under attack.

"After a little while, she saw a man named Fontaine and his family coming down the river in a canoe. They were paddling like crazy, trying to get to the fort. Madeleine asked the two soldiers, La Bonté and Gachet, to go down to the river and meet the canoe and help the people into the fort. Nothing doing. They were too scared. They'd been too scared to go up on the ramparts and fire the cannon, too. So, once again, Madeleine did what had to be done herself. She told people afterwards that she was hoping the Iroquois would figure all this moving around outside the fort was intended to lure the warriors into an ambush. It turns out that is just what the Iroquois thought, and so they didn't attack. Madeleine marched Fontaine and his whole family ahead of her into the fort just as easily as if they were walking home from a picnic. There now were six people there with her who could shoot: her brothers, the old man, Laviolette, Fontaine, and another who was with Fontaine—his oldest child, I think. It was getting dark, so she sent three of the six to guard the blockhouse where she'd shut up the women and children. She'd decided the soldiers were absolutely hopeless, so they were shut in there, too. Then she, her brothers, and the old man went to guard the rest of the fort. They made a lot of noise, shouting 'All's well' to each other and generally sounding as if the fort was full of soldiers. Toward dawn, they heard what was left of the cattle coming back from the fields. It was many hours after time for their evening milking. They let the cattle into the fort, too—hoping there weren't any Iroquois following them.

"By the next morning, everything was pretty much in order, except for Marguerite, Fontaine's wife. She was from Paris and must have been a real sissy. She kept asking her husband to carry her to another fort. I wonder where she thought he'd find one! Anyway, Fontaine told everybody he wouldn't leave Madeleine, and Madeleine wasn't going anywhere. She didn't even eat or sleep for two whole days.

"They were there like that for a week, every minute expecting the Iroquois to find out how few of them there were and attack. On the last night Madeleine was dozing—just resting at a table with her head down. She still had her gun across her arms. Anyway, her sentries came and told her there were voices on the river. When she went to investigate, it turned out to be a troop of Frenchmen. They were sneaking up on the fort because they were afraid the Iroquois might be holding it. Of course Madeleine let them in. When the French lieutenant—a man named La Monnerie—looked around, he said later that the fort was as orderly as if there'd been a whole army stationed there. Madeleine turned command over to him just as if she'd been another lieutenant greeting a relief column. She recommended that her sentries be changed, since they'd been on duty for a week."

Marie-Thérèse stopped talking.

"Holy Ste. Ursula!" Anne breathed.

"Yes indeed," agreed Marie Therese. "And that's not all, either," Marie-Thérèse grinned. "She even saved the laundry!"

Their own laundry dried and folded, the two young women headed back into the house. Marie-Thérèse paused to unhook the baby from his spot on the wall. "I'd like you to come with me tonight to Michel's," she said to Anne. "I'm going to need some moral support."

"I'll be glad to go, but I can't imagine your needing my support in anything," Anne looked puzzled.

"Trust me. I'll need you tonight. I'm going to break the news to Michel and Annette that I'm taking the children and going to Montreal."

Anne dropped down on the nearest chair with a plop. "You're WHAT? Why? When?"

"Because Antoine needs supplies at the fort at Michilimackinac, and these idiots in government can't even agree that he should be there, much less supply him efficiently. His letters sound as if he's exhausted, trying to keep up with politics and Indians both, and the Jesuit missionaries are driving him mad. I know that I can organize a house. There's no reason why I can't organize shipments of supplies. Antoine and Governor Frontenac are good enough friends that the governor knows me a little. I'm sure that he will let me ship things to my husband, and he doesn't need to know that I'm managing the purchasing, too. Actually, I'm going to begin before I ask him. Then I'll only need permission to keep on doing something that I've already made successful. I know Antoine's business contacts. They'll think I am acting as his agent, and I am. If I have to, I'll just remind everybody that I'm related to the Duc de Lauzon, but I don't think I'll need to go that far."

Marie-Thérèse went on talking. Much of what she said Anne already knew, but it helped to hear it all put together.

In the year following Phips's attack on Port Royal, she explained, Antoine had come home from Fort de Buade. The damage to the property in Port Royal took time to repair—longer than it might have done because political concerns took up so much of his time. Then, early in 1692, *petit* Antoine was born. Once he was certain that all was well, the senior Antoine Cadillac kissed his wife and new son good-bye and crossed the ocean to Paris. There, he gained audience at the palace of Versailles. He had a new idea—one that could simplify the defense of New France.

"Antoine told King Louis and his court that it wouldn't take much—just a few small ships in the lakes and lighter boats to patrol the main rivers," Marie-Thérèse explained. "The king appointed Count Pontchartrain to hear him, but Count Pontchartrain just listened politely and then sent Antoine back here to help Jean-Baptiste Franquelin make maps of New England. Maybe the maps were to provide evidence that the north country can be protected by a navy patrolling the waterways to the south. I don't know. In any case, Antoine went up and down the New England coast while I fixed up the house in Port Royal. When Madeleine came along, Antoine was back home just long enough for Governor Frontenac to appoint him captain of the marines."

"I thought he made him an ensign in the navy," Anne interrupted.

"That too!" Marie grinned. "He did that at the same time." She went on. Once Antoine had been given official military rank, it was logical for Governor Frontenac to appoint him to command of the fort at Michilimackinac. The old commandant, Sieur la Porte de Louvigny, had asked to return to Paris on business, and who better to hold down a post in the west than Cadillac, who had always pressed for its exploration? At least so Governor Frontenac thought.

"Michilimackinac is a good fort," Marie continued. "Antoine wrote me right away saying that his soldiers are very well trained. There are sixty houses inside the fort, and over two hundred good men. The problem is that he has to sort out over thirty native tribes, each of which always seems to be at war with somebody else. There are more chiefs than tribes, and the chiefs argue with each other, too. Antoine told Governor Frontenac that *'the commander of [Michilimackinac] ought always to keep a watchful eye, ready to deal with anything.'* And that's what he's been doing. Now I've found a way that I can help him."

⚜   ⚜   ⚜

"Because I can help my husband that way!" Marie-Thérèse was almost shouting. It had been an excellent idea to bring Anne with her to Michel and Annette's house. The discussion became more and more heated over supper. Finally Anne gathered all five children and took them back home to tuck them into bed in relative quiet, leaving Marie-Thérèse to do battle alone with her brother and sister-in-law.

"You can't forbid me," Marie-Thérèse said for the tenth time. "Antoine has already told the Governor that I will be coming, and that I am to be treated as his *commissaire*. I have been appointed by my husband to buy such equipment and provisions as he needs." Marie-Thérèse crossed her fingers under the table. Maybe it wasn't a lie. Antoine could have said such a thing, couldn't he?

At last, Marie-Thérèse won her case. Annette despaired over the babies—"dragged off to a strange place," as she said—but Michel promised to book passage for Marie-Thérèse and all the children on the next ship headed for Montreal. He still hesitated, but he reassured himself that there wasn't much trouble that even Marie-Thérèse could get into right there under the eye of the governor. After all, it wasn't as if she were going off into the wilderness, or something like that.

Once in Montreal, to everyone's surprise but her own and Antoine's, Marie-Thérèse turned out to be a very efficient *commissaire*. She bought goods at the best possible prices and managed to ship them to a delighted Antoine just before—but not too much before—they were needed. She could and did relieve him of at least one important worry. Unfortunately, she could do little to help him in his struggles with the Jesuits.

Marie-Thérèse remembered well how strict the Jesuit priests had been during her days in the monastery. The Ursuline sisters worked and prayed all day long in accordance with their rule, but they still laughed and had fun much like an overlarge family. The Jesuits, just next door, had seemed stern and unsmiling. The priests worked just as hard for God, and they did wonderful things in their hospital. But all the time they acted as though, if they set even one foot wrong, they would meet with some terrible punishment. If the priests were trying to treat Antoine as strictly as the ones next door to the monastery had treated themselves, Marie-Thérèse could understand his frustration with them.

It was Antoine's idea to gather as many tribes as he could to the fort at Michilimackinac. The priests were right there, he told people; they could teach the warriors about Christianity and teach them the French language at the same time. Most importantly, if all the tribes were there together, Antoine reasoned, he could trade for furs much more easily than if they were scattered.

In general, Antoine's idea worked well. All the tribes were eager to trade the best beaver pelts for brandy. Brandy was easy to get and cheap to trade. Antoine looked away when various warriors, drinking that brandy, sometimes did things they should not do. As long as he could keep the tribes from going to war with each other and endangering the fur trade, he figured that anything else they did was not his concern. But the Jesuits were unhappy. Their mission was to go into the wilderness itself, carrying the word of God to the native villages. They did not think the tribes should be brought in close contact with French civilization. Most of all, they did not believe brandy ever should be given to any warrior in any tribe—for any reason.

"Al-soom-se would agree with that," Marie-Thérèse told Jacques as she changed his clothing for the fourth time that morning. "She didn't like the Jesuit priests much—at least not as much as the Récollets—but she saw her brother once after he'd had some of a trader's brandy. He was still a boy, and it didn't take much to make him drunk—just a couple of big swallows. He got really silly. He told Al that he was the fiercest and bravest warrior in all the Abenaki territory. He may have felt that way, but, from what Al told me, he was wobbling around so much that he couldn't have shot a small rabbit if it was holding still. There!" she finished, giving her son a pat on the behind. "Stay dry until after I give your sisters their lessons."

As the months went on, fashion changed. Fewer furs were worn in Paris. It became harder and harder to find a market for the beautiful pelts Antoine shipped back to Montreal. And, of course, with the fur trade slowing, the Jesuits had more and more to say about what should be done at Michilimackinac. Worried because Antoine's letters sounded increasingly desperate, Marie-Thérèse asked for a second audience with Governor Frontenac.

"It is always a pleasure to see you, Madame," Count Louis de Buade Frontenac was always gracious, but today there was an extra twinkle in his eye. "Never fear. I shall continue to defend your husband from the church. I have faith in his ability, and I do not hesitate to tell anyone so who asks. But things do seem a bit touchy just now. Has he told you about this?" Frontenac tossed a letter toward Marie-Thérèse. She knew the handwriting well.

"I tell you, Monsieur," she read, *"that I almost forgot that [Father Carheil] was a priest, and was on the point of breaking his jaw. But, thanks be to God, I contented myself by taking him by the arm, and leading him out of the fort, telling him to stay out of it in the future."*

"Oh dear," Marie-Thérèse looked up in dismay. "He hadn't told me quite that much, but I knew it was bad. This man Carheil—he's been taking people aside in private and trying to turn them against Antoine."

"I gathered as much," replied Frontenac dryly. "I know that Lamothe—your Antoine, always 'Lamothe' to me, I'm afraid—has written to friends complaining because I've not given him permission to leave Michilimackinac. But he's the best man I can put there in a difficult situation. I've needed him. The fur trade will pick up again, and his methods—whether they are popular or not—guarantee us a steady supply of pelts. Still, I think I will have good news for him soon. He does not yet know that on the first of May, His Majesty Louis XIV ordered us to withdraw from our western forts. I'm not sure what His Majesty is thinking—but he's ordered us to cut our Western presence. It's 1697. We've been there for a decade. It's probably money—everything is.

"We can't pull out right away. It will take some time to do so in an orderly fashion." Marie-Thérèse started to speak, and Frontenac lifted a hand to silence her. "Even without your asking me, Madame, I think I can promise that your husband will be home before the end of the summer."

The traitorous words "For how long?" flashed through Marie-Thérèse's mind, but she began to smile. "That's good news, indeed, Monsieur." Her smile grew broader. Marie-Thérèse tried to sound gracious and poised, but she felt like she was ready to explode. "If you keep me informed about Antoine's timetable, I will be careful not to oversupply his men," she finished—very properly. She managed to say all the other polite things that needed to be said, made her curtsy, and swept grandly out of the governor's great hall. Once she was out the governor's sight, she stopped. She hugged her elbows to her sides with either hand— then threw her arms wide and spun and spun and spun down the hall. A startled sentry stepped back from the exit door, tripping over his sword and musket as he did so. They clattered against each other in time with Marie-Thérèse's flying feet.

"Don't worry, *chéri,*" Marie-Thérèse said to him impishly as she danced past him. "It's not an attack of anything. I always behave like this when my husband is coming home!"

❧ 15 ❧

A New Way to Protect the Fur Trade

Governor Frontenac's word was good, and August of 1697 brought Antoine back to Québec. His voice boomed out even before he reached the house. "Where is my *commissaire?* I am here. I need food. I need shelter. Where is my *commissaire?* Some good you are, Thérèse!" he finished with mock scorn.

Marie-Thérèse, breathless, threw open the front door. He was early—days earlier than she had expected him. There must have been a ship coming downriver sooner than either had hoped. "Ooof!" she gasped. "Antoine! Put me down! Put me down, I say! The neighbors!" for Antoine had picked her up and now held her at arms length above his head.

"Hang the neighbors," Antoine laughed. "Let them think it's just another of your wild Abenaki ways." But he set her back on her feet, planting a smacking kiss on her lips as he did so.

Separations weren't that steep a price to pay for homecomings like this, Marie-Thérèse thought that evening. Long after bedtime, she and Antoine sat together in the front parlor of the little house, just as if he had never left home. The children had been sent upstairs hours before. The room was pitch dark. On this hot night, there was no fire—and Antoine stopped her when she started to light the lamps. "They'll just make the room hotter," he explained. But Marie-Thérèse guessed at another reason that her husband didn't want to be surrounded by lamplight.

"Let's go outside," she spoke her thoughts aloud. "Let's walk down to the river. We can talk there as easily as here. And the air will be fresher—and maybe a bit cooler near the water. There will be less of civilization around you. I don't think it's the heat that's bothering you. You're just feeling trapped by the city."

Antoine stood up quickly. "That's why I married you, Thérèse," he smiled, extending an arm to assist her from her chair. "I knew from the moment you spoke that night at Denonville's ball—you would always understand what I was thinking. We don't belong here in Québec, either of us. One day soon we'll both go. . . ."

Marie-Thérèse laid a hand against his lips. "Don't make promises, Antoine. I understand why I must wait here now, but I will promise you one thing. When the time is right for me to see the land of the Huron, not you nor anyone else will stop me."

Now, why had she said that, she wondered to herself. She sounded almost as if they were arguing. She stole a glance at Antoine. Either he hadn't entirely heard her, or she'd said something of the kind so often he hadn't noticed. At least he still was smiling.

Quietly, the two stole out into the night. "Why are we both tiptoeing like this?" giggled Marie-Thérèse. "It's only the dogs that have to be indoors by nine o'clock."

Antoine made no reply, but continued to move silently across the cobbles. All right. Maybe he was playing a game. Maybe he was just busy thinking. Or maybe—and Marie-Thérèse nodded to herself at the thought—he just shared her feeling that this first night together again was something fragile, something that shouldn't be interrupted with the wrong words at the wrong time.

Their house wasn't far from the Château—one of the few houses in Upper Town. They had a longish walk to the stairs to Lower Town, and then down to the waterfront. By the time they reached the level of the river, the night was not so silent. The river had a sound all its own—a constant soft rushing that was felt more than heard. Here, people were out and about . . . and they were not people who felt it at all necessary to be quiet. The doors to the taverns were open, and late-night drinkers stood in the streets to avoid the heat of crowded taprooms. Voices called out, some angry, some querulous—whiny and complaining—all of them overloud. Marie-Thérèse heard a woman laugh.

"Do you feel like walking more?" Antoine asked.

For answer, Marie-Thérèse stuck out one foot. Instead of satin house-slippers, she was wearing a pair of moccasins.

"Good! Let's get away from here!" Antoine took her hand and pulled her along behind him as if she were a small child. Over the dockyard clutter and past the buildings at the outer edge of Lower

Town, they made their way—silent again, turning often just to grin at each other.

They headed upstream. Soon the rush of the water began to carry the noise of the town away from them. At first there were only a few houses ahead of them, and then there was nothing. A few more steps and the cliff came right down to the water's edge.

"This is it, I think," Antoine spoke into the silence. "And here, I believe, is our new front parlor!" Trees grew against the cliff, twisting and turning in an attempt to cling to the steep slope. Two of these had twisted in opposite directions, their trunks bent into two bench-like seats. There was just enough room for two people to sit there—if they sat very closely. Antoine lifted Marie-Thérèse to one end of the "chair" and then scrambled to his own seat.

"You'll ruin your shirt and breeches," Marie-Thérèse worried.

"And you've already ruined your dress. Never mind. I can afford others," he smiled, his teeth gleaming for an instant in the moonlight.

"We need to talk, Thérèse. You know how concerned I am for the fur trade. The English are not stupid. They've let the French control much of the trade because they still are able to obtain furs through New York. But this will not last forever, and there's a larger problem. We need a place from which we can run the fur trade like a business—where we can keep too many beaver skins from coming to market all at once."

Marie-Thérèse understood. The daughter of a merchant, she knew that if there were too many beaver skins available, the price would go down.

Antoine was still talking. "I've found the place to do it, Thérèse. Denonville knew of it, and the English certainly do. There is a spot where Huron and Érié—the two most important of the great waters—come together. The water is narrow where they meet—a true strait, *le détroit*. If we were to build a fort there, we could keep the English out of the Northwest. Their exploration would be stopped right there. We'd have all the fur trade to the North and the Northwest of *le détroit*—as far as a man can travel. And the lake of the Hurons and the waters to the North and West lead to the valley of the Mississippi. You only have to follow them far enough. And the Mississippi connects us again to New France, far to the south. A fort at *le détroit* protects all of this. It even protects our native allies in the West from the tribes of the Five Nations." Antoine waved his hands to emphasize what he was saying.

116

GOVERNOR FRONTENAC. Although Governor Louis de Buade de Frontenac was older than Antoine de Lamothe Cadillac, the two men were good friends. This picture of a statue of Frontenac was first printed in the *Dominion Illustrated News* in 1891, over a hundred years ago. It shows the energy and determination that made Frontenac one of Canada's greatest early governors. He's wearing full uniform, ready to do battle with the Iroquois or the English. (Louis Philippe Hébert, *Statue of Frontenac,* National Archives of Canada, C-007183.)

"What does the governor say about this?" Marie-Thérèse asked, ducking as a particularly broad gesture almost hit her.

"Pardon, Thérèse," Antoine said absently. "Frontenac is completely in agreement with me. He knows that Michilimackinac is not enough, does not give us the power we need. He, I—we are both angry that King Louis calls his soldiers back from the western forts. It makes no sense to us." He paused. The water rushed by below their feet—a little nearer, a little higher than it had been a few minutes before. Even this far inland, the tides could be felt.

"Ah. I see. And when will you go to Paris this time?" Marie-Thérèse asked in a small, stifled voice.

"Oh no, Thérèse! Don't sound like that. I am home, *chérie.* Yes, I may have to go one day and talk to the king myself, but not—not until we have sent the right dispatches. Not until we have shown him what is obvious. He must agree to what is common sense!"

Marie-Thérèse took a deep breath. "You're right. I know it's common sense, and I know I'm selfish to whimper when you talk of going to Paris. If you must go to see the king, you will. But you also are right about being home. Tonight, right now, husband mine—you are back home with me." Marie-Thérèse leaned her head on Antoine's shoulder and permitted herself a small sigh of contentment.

It may have sounded like common sense to Marie-Thérèse, but to Louis XIV, wearily dealing with dispatch after dispatch, this particular kind of common sense was far too expensive. In his fifties, Louis was no longer a young man. He would not live forever, and he felt a need to put his kingdom in order and keep it that way. No, Louis thought. This was not the time to throw yet more money into a land most Frenchmen would never see.

So, in New France, the year dragged by. The property in Port Royal demanded his time, but Antoine spent many hours talking, talking—in Montreal and in Québec—wherever he could find anyone who might support the idea of a fort at *le détroit.*

Then, early in December of the following winter, Antoine walked stiffly up the stairs from Lower Town. No ships traveled to Montreal and back this late in the year, but Abenaki and Algonquin runners and the *coureurs de bois* still brought news, whether it was welcome news or not. Often the most recent word could be heard in the taverns, long before official messengers reached the Château St. Louis. So it had been this day. It wasn't snowing any more, though it had snowed all that day. It was cold outside—cold enough that Antoine's feet felt numb in his boots. The fires at home would feel good, but today there was a cold inside him that the fire would not touch. He opened his front door and stood in the foyer, dripping slightly on the floor. "Thérèse?" he called.

"Oui. Ici! Yes, here!" she answered, coming into the hall. "What is it?"

"He's dead. Frontenac's dead. For over a week now."

"Oh NO! That marvelous old man! How? Was it just age?"

Marie-Thérèse disconnected Jacques from her skirts where he clung. "Go! Go play with Madeleine and the others." She came to stand before her husband. He had not yet unbuttoned his heavy winter cape. She did it for him, hanging it on one of the clothes hooks that lined the foyer.

"That and illness," Antoine replied. "He was sick for quite a while, and by the last few weeks, he knew it was his last illness. He had the Récollets with him, not the Jesuits." Antoine smiled wryly. "He made his peace with everybody else, but he still knew how to pick his priests."

"How old . . ." began Marie-Thérèse.

"Seventy-eight," Antoine said quickly. "A good age, but all the same, he held his office like a young man. We've lost a lot. But there is one thing that will make you smile, Thérèse. Do you remember how Madame Frontenac resented the time her husband gave to New France?"

"I certainly do!" replied Marie-Thérèse. "That woman. . . ." She deliberately left her sentence unfinished.

"Well," Antoine went on with something of his old twinkle in his eyes, "Frontenac left most of his fortune to her. He gave some gifts to other friends, but she got the bulk of it. Then he ordered that his heart be removed and put in a case of lead and silver and sent to her. He meant for her to bury it in his family tomb. But she wouldn't take it. She told everybody that she had never had his heart when he was living, and she didn't want it when he was dead!"

"That woman!" said Marie-Thérèse again, laughing out loud. Antoine chuckled with her, and then stopped, sober again.

"Now I really must go back to France, Thérèse. You know that?

Marie-Thérèse nodded.

❦ 16 ❦
Changes

"I never thought I'd say this, but I am honestly glad that Antoine's gone to France. He's been so miserable here since Frontenac died. At least now he feels like he's accomplishing something." Marie-Thérèse kicked off her fashionable shoes and propped her feet on the seat of a gilded dining chair. "Don't tell Antoine I did that," she added. "For that matter, you can tell Antoine, if you like. But don't you dare tell Annette!"

"Here," Anne Picoté moved to the chair and sat on it, lifting Marie-Thérèse's feet into her lap. "I'll rub them for you. You look tired—and who wouldn't be, with those five underfoot." She nodded toward the back garden, where happy shrieks could be heard as the children splashed in puddles left by the morning's rain. Anne knew well what it could mean to keep house for a growing family.

"It's not numbers one through five that wear me out. It's number six." Marie-Thérèse patted her stomach. "I haven't felt as well with this one."

"Well, it'll be here soon enough—and wearing you out in a different way. When is Annette coming to stay with you?" Anne shifted slightly in order to rub Marie-Thérèse's other foot.

"Tomorrow, actually. The baby isn't due for another week, but you never know for certain—and I've been so tired lately.

"It's just been everything, really," Marie-Thérèse went on. "We miss Governor Frontenac terribly. Governor de Callières is all pomp and show. Ever since Frontenac's death, he's spent most of his time demanding that the world treat him like some kind of a prince. And he doesn't really support Antoine. Do you remember Monsieur de Champigny? The man who is so loud in his support of the Jesuits? He called a meeting where he and de Callières both attacked Antoine at once. They don't want a fort at *le détroit* because they know that, if one is built, it will be run Antoine's way. Among other things, they just won't accept that it will be a good thing to teach French to the people who live there. Instead, the Jesuits spend all their time writing dictionaries and learning to speak Algonquin or Abenaki or Iroquois. . . ." She sputtered and stopped.

"I think it's more than that, Marie-Thérèse," Anne said. "Think about it. If a fort to the south is successful, Michilimackinac will go away. It just won't be needed any more. And the Jesuit missionaries there might not be needed either. At least they wouldn't have the protection of the fort as they do now. I think this is an old-fashioned struggle for power and territory, and Antoine has made some powerful enemies among the Jesuits."

"Well, no one has more power than the king, and that's who Antoine is counting on to settle this." Marie-Thérèse stood up and winced as she jammed her feet back into her shoes. "OH!" She sat back down again.

"What is it? Your feet?" Anne asked, startled by the volume of the last word.

"No, not my feet. My back. And it's not just a cramp. Anne, I've been trying to ignore it all day. I really did think I was just very tired. But now, I guess you'd better go fetch Annette right away—and have her bring the midwife when she comes."

Anne stepped forward to help her friend, but Marie-Thérèse waved her away. "No," she said. "I'm really all right, but I don't think there's much time. Go get Annette. She wants to watch the children and run the house for me this time. If you can't find the midwife, come back yourself. I can manage without the midwife if I have to. It won't be the first time. But it will help if you are here." She finished with a small grimace of pain. "Hurry?"

Anne fairly flew out the door.

Two very important things arrived in Québec the next morning. The first was a loudly yelling young man, very red of face and black of hair. "Pierre Denis," said Marie-Thérèse to Annette, introducing her to the baby. "After Michel Denis and after our father."

The second arrival was a messenger carrying a letter from Antoine. A sailor, he beat on the front door and stood there impatiently. Ashore in Québec for the first time, there were things he would rather do than deliver letters. He was a little bewildered. He could hear many people moving around in the house, yet no one answered his knock. He pounded on the door again. At last and with difficulty, Anne tore herself away from Marie-Thérèse and the new baby. She came down the stairs and opened the door, hardly looking to see who was standing there. Vaguely, she realized that a figure held out a letter. She took one glance at the handwriting and started back up the stairs to Marie-Thérèse. Then she remembered the messenger. She turned back quickly.

"I'm so sorry," Anne said. "You should be rewarded for bringing this. You'd best go through to the kitchen. For your trouble, tell Claudette that I said you were to have a full meal—with fresh vegetables. I'd have said so straightaway, but we've already had our share of excitement here this morning," she explained.

"*Merci! Merci!* Thank you Madame!" The sailor hurried off toward the kitchen. He needed only follow his nose to go in the right direction. The whole house was filled with the warm scent of fresh-baked bread. His stomach rumbled in anticipation.

As tired as she was after a night without sleep, Anne made it up the stairs with Antoine's letter in almost a single step. She spun through the door of the bedroom where Marie-Thérèse lay in the big four-poster—the blanket-wrapped morsel that was Pierre snuggled warmly under her chin.

"From Antoine?"

Anne nodded, and held out the letter. Marie-Thérèse took it in her hands and just held it for a moment. "From your father," she murmured to the baby. "He's sending his new son greetings." She smiled and handed the paper back to Anne.

"Go on, Anne. You read it to all of us," she said. "I'm too tired to sit up that long. Antoine never says anything that personal, anyway."

"Are you sure?" Anne took the letter and moved to the window where the light was better. Marie-Thérèse nodded. "All right, then." Anne broke the seal.

"'My dear Thérèse,'" she read aloud. "'I cannot tell you with what pleasure I sit down to write this letter—a pleasure that Monsieur de Champigny most certainly will not share with me. It has happened at last! King Louis has given us fifteen arpents of

THE DUC DE LAUZUN. The only accurate picture of Marie-Thérèse has been lost since 1731, but maybe she looked something like the Duc de Lauzun, who was related to her mother's family. Here he is wearing the English "Order of the Garter." If you look carefully, you can see that he has been made a knight of St. George. A tiny statue of St. George killing the dragon hangs from the chain across his chest. The picture also gives us a very good idea of how people dressed in the court of Louis XIV. The silk and satin outfit is painted so perfectly, it's easy to imagine what it looked and felt like. The Duc's large, soft periwig probably was very warm. Many men shaved their heads or cut their hair short so that their wigs would be more comfortable. (Godfrey Kneller ["d'après," 1646–1723, Great Britain], *Antoine-Nompar de Caumont, duc de Lauzun (1633–1723)*. Saumur, Mus. des Arts Decoratifs. Photo by Lauros-Giraudon, RL 17288.)

land on which to build a fort at *le détroit*, and he has given me his blessing to build it.'

"I'm no good at measuring land," Anne frowned. "That's a lot, isn't it?"

"Don't you remember the time that Mother St. Esprit made us walk out an arpent and compare it to an English acre? She said it was in case our husbands ever bought land from the English. They were about the same. Fifteen arpents—maybe twelve or thirteen English acres. . . . Oh, Anne! That's a great deal. Enough land for a fort and several small fields to plant for food. What else does he say?" Marie-Thérèse propped herself up on one elbow. Tiny Pierre grunted a little in complaint.

"'I met many times with Count Pontchartrain, the minister of colonies. He tells me that it was money alone that kept him from acting on my suggestion that we build a light fleet to protect the waterways of New France. Since land is free, the cost to the court is in men and supplies. His Majesty finds it easier to support a fort than to support ships that have to be built. Or at least I think that is what the good Count was telling me.

"'The best news is that His Majesty has issued a *mémoire*—a command—and sent it to both our good Governor de Callières and to Monsieur de Champigny. They are to gather leading citizens and landowners, and all that they gather are to listen to me, not to them. These people are supposed to decide whether the fort should be built, based on what I and I alone tell them. De Callières is to report the result of the meeting to the court. The king finishes by saying that, as far as construction of the fort is concerned, *they will have the permission of His Majesty.* Thérèse, *mon amour,* we have won!

"'By the time this letter reaches you, I will not be many days away from you. I must go first to Montreal, and then return to Québec to meet with these "leading citizens." I hope that, when I come to Québec, I may find you well—and perhaps with a new arrival to introduce to me.'

"That's all he's written, Marie-Thérèse. Except, of course, he signs his name."

"All? Oh, Anne, that is everything. That is what we have both wanted ever since our marriage—to go beyond the land of the Huron. And this time, we will both go there. I know it!" Marie-Thérèse fell back on her pillows, but she no longer looked as if she needed them. Her face glowed as she thought of the preparations to come.

❧   ❧   ❧

The next year passed quickly. Then yet another summer came and went—but almost without Marie-Thérèse's noticing, there was so much to do. Another new baby hung in her cradle-board on the wall now—a little girl this time, named Marie Anne. "How do you decorate that spot when you don't have a baby to put there?" teased Antoine, kissing the back of Marie-Thérèse's neck as he walked past her to the dining table.

To someone who did not know the Cadillacs, the scene in the dining area of the house in Québec would have looked like any household after mealtime. The children, served separately, had been taken away for their naps—all but the baby. Marie-Thérèse kept this baby near her. Marie Anne was bouncing and healthy—not like Pierre. "Poor Pierre," Marie-Thérèse thought, sighing.

Pierre had not grown as rapidly as the other children. His little arms stayed thin, and his head seemed almost too heavy for his neck to hold up. When he was almost a year old, he still could not walk on his own. Then one day, not all that long after Marie Anne's birth, Marie-Thérèse heard Pierre whimper. He'd been fretful and feverish all day—cutting a tooth, Marie-Thérèse thought, and she rubbed his gums hard with her finger to help it come through. But he pushed her hand away. "Be that way, then, Pierre," she smiled, kissed his forehead, and put him back down to sleep.

Afterward she told Antoine she was not gone from the room more than a minute—just long enough to see that Judith had come back from an errand to town. "Good, dependable Judith," she said. Pierre was quiet when she went back to check on him. Too quiet. When she picked him up, she knew.

Other mothers lost babies all the time. All the ladies Marie-Thérèse knew marveled at the health of the Lamothe Cadillac children. She never thought she'd have a child that would die. But now it had happened, and there was nothing she could do about it—except keep Marie Anne close to her.

Antoine sat at the great dining table. It was covered with paper and writing materials. In front of him, the afternoon sunlight shone on a map of New France.

"De Callières may be an idiot, but he's no fool when it comes to protecting his own interests," Antoine remarked to Marie-Thérèse as she came to join him. "He wants to be seen as agreeing with the king, so now he tells people that he 'strongly approves' of building the fort. Even when he objects, he's got it down to two complaints. He's afraid the Iroquois will drive off the friendly tribes, and then he's afraid the friendly tribes will trade their beaver to the English. Not one word about whether or not they all live near the fort or out in the wilderness, and not one word about whether or not they should speak French or be paid in brandy. He's made it official, you know. He sent word to the court that—" Antoine broke off. "Well, here. Here's a copy. See for yourself!"

Marie-Thérèse looked at the paper he held. It was dated October 17, 1700. Written just that past week, she thought. It was not in de Callières's handwriting. Some young courtier had made the copy, and it was smudged and hard to read. She squinted at the paper. *"In the spring,"* it read, *"I will send sieur de Lamothe with sieur de Tonty to build a fort at [le] détroit. My plan is to send them to take possession of this post on the shores of the Lake of the Hurons by way of the Ottawa River, thereby avoiding the passage of Niagara in order not to give offense to the Iroquois."*

"His plan indeed!" Marie-Thérèse huffed. "So, what are you writing now? A defense of the Iroquois?" Marie-Thérèse was joking, but she leaned closer to see what Antoine had on the paper before him.

"There's nothing here yet, really," Antoine answered her. "Actually, I'm putting down what we need to do to make this fort at *le détroit* a success. Most of it I think you know already. We've got to start out with at least a hundred men, half of them soldiers, or else we'll be easy targets for the English. We've talked about that. After we've been at *le détroit* for a year, I'd like to get in about twenty or thirty families of settlers—farmers and their sheep and cattle—and another couple hundred young men who are tradesmen and craftsmen."

Marie-Thérèse sat down. "You intend to build a city, not just a fort, don't you?"

Antoine chuckled. "You know me far too well, Thérèse. We have to make this fort into the Québec of the West—the furthest west in New France that one can find real civilization. That way, King Louis will never lose interest in us.

"We'll have missionaries, of course—to teach all the tribes French, so that we can use that language to teach them civilization. Just teaching the religion isn't enough. We have to teach them about the law. Your Ursulines can come in about the third year—maybe the fourth. Somebody, the Ursulines or some other sisters, will need to help us in the hospital. We should set up a hospital as soon as possible. Taking care of a man when he's hurt is about the best way to gain his friendship, and that's as true with an Iroquois as it is with an Abenaki—or a Frenchman."

Marie-Thérèse reached across the table to take Antoine's hand. "Do you still plan to have the soldiers marry Abenaki and Ottawa girls? Will the girls want to marry someone outside of their tribes?" she asked earnestly.

"Now what girl would marry a native when she could marry a Frenchman like me? Or even like Alphonse de Tonty?" Antoine demanded indignantly.

"I believe you're half serious," laughed Marie-Thérèse, "as well as being arrogant. I'm sure there are many warriors as fine as either of you."

"I am serious, Thérèse. The native women I've known are more than eager to marry the French. You'll see. It will help cement the friendship of the tribes, too."

"I wonder if it really will work that way," Marie-Thérèse worried aloud. "I think your Frenchmen are going to miss their mothers and sisters and want to marry women more like the ones that they knew at home. Just as I, no matter how many friends I have among the Abenaki, would always prefer to marry someone who reminded me of my family."

"Someone like me, I hope," said Antoine dryly. "Hand me that quill, would you? This pen is getting blunt."

127

✣ 17 ✣

Bon Voyage to Détroit

It was May again. Always things seemed to begin in May, and for
Marie-Thérèse and Antoine, this May looked as if it could be
the greatest beginning of all. It certainly felt that way to nine-
year-old *petit* Antoine. He could scarcely contain himself. He ran
back and forth across the pier—now scrambling to the top of a
pile of luggage, now tightrope walking the tongue of a wagon.

"These are fallen tree trunks. It's the only way I can cross the
swamp and escape the Iroquois," he gasped, leaping from cobblestone to cobblestone where they bridged the ruts wagons had left
in the street.

"Better quit that, or Papa will leave you here in Québec and
take me with him instead," Joseph warned.

"No he won't, Joseph. You have to stay here and look after
Mama and Jacques and the girls, because you're the oldest. I
heard Papa say. 'At eleven Joseph is old enough to do a man's
work,' he said—and that means staying here and being the man
of the family while Papa is gone."

Marie-Thérèse heard the shrill voices. "Antoine!" she said in
a tone that made it perfectly clear which Antoine she meant.
"Antoine! Young man, you come here this minute."

"*Oui,* Mama? What do you want?" The same feet that had
been flying before dragged a little as their owner—trying desperately to look innocent—approached Marie-Thérèse.

"What do I want?" Marie-Thérèse snapped, "I want this departure for Montreal to go smoothly. We don't have time to take care
of you if you get into trouble. It's very simple: if you fall and hurt
yourself, you and Joseph both will stay with me. If you make your

father angry, you might get left with me anyway. Show some sense! I know you are excited, but you need to start acting like the man your father plans to take with him on this trip—not some little boy who should stay at home with his mother and sisters."

"*Oui,* Mama," *petit* Antoine said again.

"See, what did I tell you?" Joseph began, and then, at a look from Marie-Thérèse, stopped himself short. "Come on," he said to his brother. "We can watch them finish loading the ship."

Marie-Thérèse bit her lip. She blamed *petit* Antoine far less than he realized. If she were the one preparing to go to Montreal with Antoine, they would need to tie her to the pier to keep her from climbing all the way to the topmast of the brig carrying her there. Because Montreal, this time, would not be the end of the voyage. Once in Montreal, Antoine and *petit* Antoine would have a few frantic weeks of equipping for their journey, and then they would head up the Ottawa River and on to *le détroit.* Today was the eighth of May. Antoine expected to be well on his way to *le détroit* by the first week of June.

"I'll be wishing I had my *commissaire* with me—every minute of the time! I can promise you that," he'd said to her that morning. "Getting all the supplies I need, and being sure that they are good quality—that's one battle I'd rather not fight."

"Don't fight it, then," Marie-Thérèse replied. "Just tell the people what you need, and send *petit* Antoine to watch them pack it and load it aboard the canoes. He knows what to look for, and people will soon find that he is your eyes."

Antoine nodded. In fact, he expected that the convenience of having his son with him would increase as the boy grew older. All the tribes were particularly conscious of family connections. *Petit* Antoine would be respected as the son of the great Chief Cadillac, a fact that could prove to be very useful.

Almost everything was in place just as Antoine had sketched it out to Marie-Thérèse the winter before. Now that it was politically convenient for de Callières to support the venture, the governor was generous with men and supplies. Antoine's party consisted of fifty soldiers, fifty *voyageurs* and settlers, and roughly a hundred men of the Abenaki, Algonquin, and other friendly tribes. To help him control this small army, he would take with him Anne's husband, Alphonse de Tonty, and two other lieutenants. And then there would be the priests. A Jesuit had been assigned to them, of

MARIE-THÉRÈSE GUYON, MME CADILLAC.
Only a few artists have tried to show
us what Marie-Thérèse may have
looked like. Here, her statue watches
over students in Marygrove College's
Madame Cadillac Hall. She is dressed
in her very finest clothing, ready for a
ball or *soirée* (important evening
gathering). In fan language, she is
telling us all that she wants to get to
know us better. (Unknown sculptor,
Mme Cadillac, Madame Cadillac Hall, Marygrove College, Detroit, Mich. Photo by Tom
Sherry.)

course. It was impossible to avoid that. The Jesuits felt they owned
every Iroquois or Ottawa, or Abenaki, or Algonquin. . . .

Antoine snorted, thinking about it. Yes, there'd be a Jesuit
with them—Father François Vaillant de Gueslis. Antoine didn't
like him, and he had a feeling Vaillant didn't care much for him
either. But Father Constantin would be there, too—Father
Bernard Constantin Delhalle. He was a Récollet, and would
understand better what Antoine was trying to do. Father
Constantin would teach the French language to any tribesman
with whom they were trading. It would be good to have Father
Constantin along.

Marie-Thérèse came over to stand with Antoine as he super-

ANTOINE LAUMET DE LAMOTHE CADILLAC. This statue by Julius Melchers stands on the campus of Wayne State University. No one knows how much it actually looks like Antoine. His portrait, like that of Marie-Thérèse, was lost long ago. But the sculptor knew how Antoine would have dressed. He has made him look as if he were ready for any adventure—with a sword in his right hand and a roll of parchment (perhaps a fur-trade agreement) in his left. (Julius Melchers [1829–1908], *Cadillac,* Wayne State University campus, Detroit, Mich. Photo by Karen Elizabeth Bush.)

vised the last of the loading of his personal goods. "I think I can keep *petit* Antoine from breaking his neck before you leave Québec," she announced by way of greeting.

"That's a good idea. I was thinking again how glad I will be to have one of my own with me this trip." Antoine reached out and took Marie-Thérèse's hand. "It's not easy, you know—always to leave you behind. But this time is different, Thérèse. This time I'll come back to fetch you—just as soon as the fort is established. This will be a real settlement, and I want you in it with me. It won't be long. A year—perhaps a year plus a month or so. That's all."

"Tell me again the route you are taking?"

Antoine grinned broadly. "Come on, Thérèse! You just like to hear the names. You've got it memorized by now!"

"When I hear them, I'm traveling there with you. Tell me," Marie-Thérèse demanded stubbornly.

"All right—de Callières decided on the northern route, you

know, and I absolutely agree. The peace treaty isn't concluded, and there's no sense in risking a confrontation with the Iroquois before we're settled in at *le détroit*. We start up the Ottawa River; you know that, too. Then we'll cross Lake Nipissing, and then take the river they call French and another named 'Pickerel,' after the fish that are found there. Then there's a great bay that connects with the Lake of the Hurons. We'll travel close to the eastern shore of the lake until we reach a river and a smaller lake— *Lac Ste. Claire*. We cross Lac Ste. Claire to another river, and that river takes us to the place called *le détroit*. It's a good long haul— about six hundred miles, and they tell me there are over thirty *portages* where the waters won't carry the canoes. We'll do a lot of walking and carrying, I'm afraid. But we'll get there."

There was a shout from the docks. Alphonse de Tonty stood waving to get Antoine's attention.

"We'll get there, and I'll come back to get you. But every journey starts with a single step, Thérèse, *mon amour*—and I need to take that step right now."

Marie-Thérèse gave him a quick hug. "Go then. Go right now—before I stow away on the ship with you." *Petit* Antoine arrived out of nowhere and stood before them, sniffling slightly. "And you too, little one," she added, bending to give her son a squeeze. "Don't you be taller than I am, now, when I see you next!" She bent down again to whisper, "Hurry! Follow your father, and don't let Joseph see you cry. I promise: you are going to be far too busy to miss us, even for a minute!"

After all that, it was an hour before the brig carrying the two Antoines and Alphonse de Tonty at last weighed anchor and started toward Montreal. Marie-Thérèse waited for the full hour, watching, and then made her way slowly to Upper Town. From the bluff, she could see the brig's masts for a long time as it beat its way upstream.

"How do you do it?" asked Anne, as she came laboring up the hill behind Marie-Thérèse.

"Do what?" Marie-Thérèse looked blank.

"Send them off like that—without a tear?" Anne's own face was swollen and blotchy from crying. "I know you care. I know you feel as strongly as I do. How do you do it?"

"I don't know," Marie-Thérèse said. "I honestly don't know. I think maybe it's that I know that Antoine thinks about me enough that I'm never far from him. And then, it's partly that I'd give anything to be doing exactly what he is doing. So how can I cry because he is doing it? There's no choice but to be happy for him. I'm ready to go home, though. I didn't think I'd be this tired, but I have to admit that I really am exhausted."

"What about Joseph?" Anne wondered. When she thought about it, she realized she hadn't seen Marie-Thérèse's "man of the family" since he'd parted company with *petit* Antoine.

"Joseph went home an hour ago. He said something about rescuing Jacques from all the girls."

"He's got that right," Anne laughed. "You did leave Jacques with a bunch of them, didn't you? And not just 'girls.' It's hard to believe that Judith is quite a young woman now—twelve years old. And Madeleine is eight. Poor Jacques! At six the only one he can boss around is the baby!"

"He'll not be able to do that for long. Marie Anne is a little tyrant! As a matter of fact, I left her with Claudette today. She'll bring her home tonight. Marie Anne is not easy to manage, and with Jacques so jealous because his brother gets to travel with Papa, I figured one spoiled baby was all I could ask Judith to worry about."

"With Claudette?" Anne looked stunned. "Marie Anne is with Claudette in Lower Town? Didn't she tell you? They had a case of measles in Lower Town last week. People are saying that the summer weather will bring another epidemic." She broke off, staring at the stricken look on Marie-Thérèse's face. "She didn't tell you? Well, maybe because it was just that one case. I'm sure the baby will be all right. Or she thought you knew. I'm sure it will be all right. . . ." Anne was babbling, and she knew it.

"Claudette will be there at the house, now. I told her to bring Marie Anne back as soon as the brig weighed anchor." Marie-Thérèse was walking faster. "She did try to tell me something this morning, but I was so busy. . . ." They were almost running now.

On June 4, 1701, Antoine Laumet de Lamothe Cadillac, his son Antoine, and a party of over two hundred soldiers, settlers, and native tribesmen left Montreal and began the long trek to *le détroit*.

Five days later, on June 9, Marie-Thérèse Guyon Cadillac stood staring at the still body of her youngest daughter and then—for the first time that her friend Anne could remember—she put her head down and wept uncontrollably.

"Come along, Joseph, Jacques, girls," Anne said softly, ushering the children before her. "Let's leave your mother alone for a while with Marie Anne."

"Oh, Madame," began Claudette, wailing.

"Hush! You too—especially you! Come along with us, Claudette. Madame doesn't blame you. She knows you tried to warn her, and she knows how much help you've been to us here— especially since the baby took sick. You've no reason to carry on. Half the children in Québec have come down with measles this month—anyway, half those who didn't have measles before. Marie Anne likely would have caught them anyway, whether or not she spent a day with you in Lower Town."

Still scolding Claudette (it was the only way to keep her from making a terrible scene), Anne led the sad little procession down the stairs and toward the back of the house. Whatever would she do with them all? Judith reached out and touched her arm. Anne turned toward her.

Around her head, Judith had wrapped one of the rags used to cover fresh bread. She tapped Anne's arm again, then reached for Madeleine's hand. She pointed to her strange headdress, and then to the door. She tapped Anne's arm a third time.

"Yes!" Anne nodded vigorously, finally understanding. "Yes, Judith. Please take Madeleine with you and go and tell the sisters. Try to find Mother Mary of the Angels, if you can. Your mother will want Mother Mary, especially, to know about Marie Anne."

Reminded of the things that needed to be done at a death, Anne turned toward Joseph.

"*Oui, Tante* Anne," Joseph didn't wait for her to speak. "I'll go for the priest."

✦ 18 ✦

Al-soom-se Takes Charge

The weather was chilly for June. Anne wrapped her cape around her more tightly. She and Al-soom-se sat huddled under the old ash tree on the monastery grounds—just as they had done over ten years before. Only now, Al-soom-se's black hair was hidden with a white veil and her schoolgirl's dress had been replaced by a nun's habit. It was the first time Anne had seen her dressed that way. Everyone knew that Al had found one reason after another not to return home to the Abenaki. Everyone knew that she spent a great deal of time helping the sisters at the Hôtel Dieu. Still, it had come as a shock when word came that Al-soom-se, whose very name meant "independent," had decided to join the Ursuline order. "I can't even call you 'Al' any more," mourned Anne, half-seriously. "You are far too dignified."

"Oh, but now everybody calls me 'Al'!" laughed Al-soom-se. "I am now Sister Denise Roy du St. Alexis. See? I am still 'Al.' At least to my friends here, I am! Even Mother Superior calls me 'Sister St. Alexis.' It's far better than being 'Denise.'"

"Are you happy, here, then?" Anne spoke in wonder—not for the first time.

"Of course I am," replied Al-soom-se. "If I wasn't, I'd just leave. For that matter, I'd not have professed as a novice. I did that on my own, and I had lots of time to think about it. It took forever to convince Uncle Pierre to give me a dowry that I could give to the monastery. You know I couldn't come here empty-handed.

"But say I went home—back to my family. I'd never be free to roam through the forest again, anyway. I'd be married. By now I'd have more children even than Marie-Thérèse." A shadow crossed her face. "Besides, the children here need me. There aren't so many Huron and Abenaki in school as there were, but when the new *petites* come in, it means so much to them to see my face. I'm just a lay sister. I don't have many of the burdens that the nuns have. I'm only here to work, and I can't turn away now. I'm needed. It's—important, somehow."

"Mother Mary was so good with the new ones, remember?" Anne mused.

Al-soom-se nodded. "She's going to be Mother Superior, did you know?"

"No, I didn't. That's wonderful."

"Al?" "Anne?" Both spoke at the same time. It was Anne who kept on speaking.

"Al, I've never seen Marie-Thérèse like this. It's not that she's moping around, exactly. She gets all the household chores done, and she's always right there for the children. Judith stays with her a lot—kind of keeps an eye on her, but even that isn't necessary, because she does all the right things.

"But?" Al-soom-se asked.

"But she's not right. She's all wrapped up in herself. There's no life, no sparkle in anything she does. She was never like this when Pierre died. The boys think she's blaming herself for Marie Anne's death, but I don't think so. She knows she had to leave Marie Anne with someone that morning, and Claudette was someone she could trust. There was nothing else she could have done. She was in Lower Town herself, anyway, saying goodbye to Antoine. If she'd kept the baby with her, it would have made no difference. So that's not it. She knows there's no reason to feel guilty. No one ever got sick in Claudette's house, anyway, so we can't even be sure that's where Marie Anne caught the disease." Anne looked at Al-soom-se with a kind of despair. "I just don't know what is wrong with her. She never had an unhappy moment with that baby. She has to realize that she gave Marie Anne as much joy in one year and two days as any infant ever had. I just don't know what is wrong with her," Anne said again.

Al-soom-se frowned. "Did she have to watch the baby suffer a lot? Maybe that is what is bothering her."

"No, not really. Marie Anne got very sick very fast. For a couple of days, she acted a little as if she had a head cold, and then she just acted sleepy. By the time we knew how hot she was, she was covered with the rash. After that, she just got quieter and quieter. She didn't have any convulsions. She finally just fell asleep and didn't wake. You can't say that she suffered, and Marie-Thérèse held her the whole time." A sudden movement caused Anne to stop talking. "Al? Where are you going?"

Al-soom-se was on her feet. "Come on, Anne," she said. "We are going to sneak out of this place one more time! We could get permission to go and see Marie-Thérèse and the children. It would not be a problem. But I've an idea that it might help Marie-Thérèse to think she's got me in trouble again."

As soon as she saw Marie-Thérèse's face, Al-soom-se knew why Anne was so worried. It wasn't just that the hollows below her cheekbones were so deep, or that the rings under her eyes were so dark. That much Al had expected. It was the severity with which her hair was pinned back, and the rigid cleanliness of her dress that looked so wrong. Al had never seen Marie-Thérèse look so adult, so proper, so . . . she didn't know what. "She looks like one of the Jesuit priests—hard on the world and harder on themselves," Al thought. She couldn't think what to say, either. She threw her arms around her friend and held her that way for a long while without speaking.

At last Al let Marie-Thérèse go. "I'm sorry I couldn't be here before now," she said. "They do keep me busy."

"Should you have come here even now?" Marie-Thérèse frowned.

"Of course not," grinned Al. "I'm sure to hear about it when I go back. But then, the Ursulines should be used to me, and they still seem to want me." Her black eyes snapped. "Do you want to help me get in *real* trouble? I haven't done the laundry in a long, long time."

Marie-Thérèse smiled a ghost of her old smile. "I'm afraid I'm not very good company these days, Al. What did you have in mind?"

Al-soom-se had done a great deal of thinking as she and Anne slipped past the gates of the monastery. Somehow she was going to have to help Marie-Thérèse focus on something or do something—something really necessary, and something that would make her so busy there'd be no time left over for anything else. And the more Al thought, the more obvious the solution became. "Leave the children with Anne and come with me, and I'll show you," she said now. "And get rid of those slippers. You'll need your moccasins, because we are going to take a little hike through the woods."

Thirty minutes later, Al turned to help Marie-Thérèse up yet another small ravine. There was no doubt about it. A religious habit was a far better costume to wear in the woods than was a silk taffeta afternoon dress—not that either outfit was particularly good for hiking. Both women were panting slightly. Al noted with pleasure that Marie-Thérèse's hair had escaped from its formal set and now blew around her face, and there even was a trace of color in her cheeks. "We're almost there," Al said. "There's only one more little bit to climb."

Al-soom-se led the way as they trudged onward. Branches caught on their skirts and held them fast. In spite of her moccasins, Marie-Thérèse tripped and fell. Suddenly Al stopped. "Look," she said, holding back a small clump of alders. The forest, a solid canopy of dark-green leaves, suddenly was not there. Marie-Thérèse gasped. There was nothing at all in front of them: no trees, no ferns, no grasses—nothing. Not even any ground that she could see. Somehow, in their climb, they'd circled behind the Hôtel Dieu and now faced back toward the river. They were not nearly as high over the river as they had been when they were in Upper Town. Yet, now that the ground dropped away from their feet, the effect was startling. Near them, a small spring leapt from the rocks and tumbled down the hill. In a matter of a few feet, the spring turned into a real stream, splashing happily and noisily as it fell toward the river. Al-soom-se dropped down on her stomach by the stream bank. "Hold my feet, Marie-Thérèse. I'm really thirsty."

Marie-Thérèse did as she was asked, gripping Al's feet firmly in her hands as Al stretched her body down the steep hill. "You next," cried Al-soom-se, laughing and snorting. She'd plunged her whole face in the stream and water dripped from her nose and chin. She grabbed for Marie-Thérèse's ankles, and Marie-Thérèse braced her hands against the hillside.

"It's not as cold as it was," she said, emerging from the stream only slightly dryer than Al-soom-se had been. "The air—not the water—I mean." Al-soom-se didn't answer. "Al?"

Marie-Thérèse had to turn around to see her. Al-soom-se was sitting upright, tailor fashion, framed by the alders that marked the forest path. She was rocking slightly to and fro, and the air around her seemed to quiver. She looked at Marie-Thérèse, and then gazed upward, staring at something that wasn't quite there.

"Do you remember my brother's story? It all begins there." As she used to do so long ago, Al-soom-se closed her eyes and rocked in rhythm with her own words. "He was young when the story begins, and very, very brave. He knew of the great waters in the lands where the sun sets, and he wanted to see them for himself. He went to the council house. He begged the wise leaders to let him go to the land of the Huron and bring back stones from the edge of the great waters. 'You may go, young brother,' the elders said. 'But before you return, remember that you must also bring back something of value to all the Abenaki—not just something for yourself.' And they asked the Great Spirit to speed him on his journey."

Just as she had done those many years before, Marie-Thérèse sat spellbound. The words of Al-soom-se's tale were familiar and soothing, and she let them flow over her—not trying to hear every word, and yet somehow hearing, understanding everything. She saw again in her mind's eye the great waters to the west. She saw glimpses of the land of the Hurons, and she thought of Antoine and *petit* Antoine—traveling to lands far beyond those that Al's brother had seen. She whispered the last words of the tale along with Al-soom-se. "They asked him what he had brought that was of value to the Abenaki. He told them this story. It will be told around the campfires of the Abenaki until the end of time," she chanted softly.

The woods were quiet when Al finished—quiet except for the noisy little stream.

"He won't send for me until next year," Marie-Thérèse said.

"I know," replied Al. "So what are you going to do about it?"

"You think I should go now, don't you?" Marie-Thérèse said in surprise. Al-soom-se did not answer. "How could I, Al? The children . . ." her voice trailed off.

Al smiled gently. "Judith loves to visit the monastery, and it's time she went to school. She knows me. I can work with her. We understand each other. There's a whole language of signs and signals made with the hands. It's used by the tribes of the Algonquin to speak to one another when they don't understand each other's words. Judith knows some of the language. I can teach her the rest. She will learn to say many things, and she'll be understood by many people—not just by her family. As for Madeleine, she is happy wherever Judith is. The boys, of course, would go with you." She paused. "You have only to follow the waters west, you know."

The little stream tumbled down the hill into the St. Lawrence River. It was going east.

"I can't follow that one," Marie-Thérèse said, laughing a little. Then she threw her head back and laughed out loud for the first time in over a month.

"Annette will have a fit!"

❊ 19 ❊

Toward the Land of the Huron

Annette did indeed have a fit. In fact she had several of them, and each one took her in a different direction. First, she railed at Michel for allowing Marie-Thérèse to associate with "that savage" (Al-soom-se). Then she attacked Anne Picoté for allowing Marie-Thérèse out of her sight and into anyone else's company when Marie-Thérèse was so obviously "disturbed of mind." She berated Marie-Thérèse herself for any number of things: for relying on Claudette, whom she called "slovenly and incompetent," to watch Marie Anne; for failing to care for the baby properly during her sickness; for her personal behavior, which was unladylike in the extreme; for marrying "that scoundrel, Cadillac." As far as any plans to travel to *le détroit* were concerned, they were almost too absurd to be considered at all—even in argument.

"For once in your life, be realistic," shrieked Annette. "You are a woman. You are alone. You have no escort. To travel that distance means keeping the company of savages, of drunken *voyageurs*. You will sleep on the ground, when you dare sleep . . . in the rains, in the wind. Canoes don't float over rocks and rapids. How do you expect to get over the *portages?* Walk? You were out of breath when you came back from walking with that savage girl. How do you expect to walk through the wilderness? Each man on a *portage* carries a hundred pounds of goods. You take up the space of a man in the canoe. Do you think you will get by without being asked to carry your share? And how do you expect to care for your children? You say you will leave your daughters with those nuns—the same ones who allowed you to associate with the kind of people who gave you this—this idea. I suppose the girls will be fed and housed well enough, even if it must be with more of your savages, but you have sons, too. Would you endanger them by dragging them along on this fool's errand? If the men who are with you don't kill you all—or worse—you'll be killed by the Iroquois. They'll attack the minute they see a defenseless party moving through their lands." Annette paused for breath, her mouth still open. Too angry to swallow or think of her own appearance, she was even drooling slightly.

Marie-Thérèse shook her head a little in wonder. She had never seen Annette this angry. "She's so wrong about *everything*. And she's actually pop-eyed when she yells like that," she thought to herself. "I wonder if she still yells at Michel, and if she looks that much like a madwoman when she does. . . ."

After weeks of attempting to match her sister-in-law's arguments, Marie-Thérèse had dropped into a pattern of just listening and watching each new attack. If nothing else, Annette's bizarre behavior was entertaining. Today Marie-Thérèse was studying the rise and fall of her sister-in-law's bodice as she drew enough breath to support the volume of her argument. With each inhalation, an ornamental pin securing her shawl moved upward. The pin had twisted slightly, and its point stood straight up. "If she opens her mouth just a little wider and breathes deep enough at the same time," Marie-Thérèse thought, "she's going to stab herself in the jaw, for sure!" She waited, half hoping for the additional howl at the moment pin met chin, but it was not to be. In the nick of time, Annette reached up and unfastened the pin, undraped the shawl, and sat herself down at Marie-Thérèse's table—all quite without invitation.

"I'm going to sit in this chair until you see reason," Annette declared. "Really, you are the most unnatural mother I have ever known. Even if you want to throw away your own life, you have no right to take those children out into trackless wilderness."

"You didn't mind when Antoine took *petit* Antoine into the same trackless wilderness," Marie-Thérèse remarked mildly.

Annette went on as if Marie-Thérèse had not spoken. "You don't even know that this Fort . . . Pontchartrain, is it? You don't even know that it's habitable. And you certainly haven't given any thought to how you are going to hire men to take you there. No Frenchman is going to do business with a woman—at least not in support of a venture like the one you are planning!"

That was the last straw. With difficulty, Marie-Thérèse kept her tone mild and sweet—certainly not because she cared what Annette thought, but because she felt her argument was a good deal stronger if she didn't stoop to Annette's level and scream like a fishwife. "You're quite right, Annette," she said, nodding her head vigorously and noting with pleasure that a sign of agreement had stopped Annette in mid-tirade.

"You're very right. That is why I have asked François-Marie Picoté de Belestre to make the arrangements on my behalf."

"François-Marie Picoté . . . What on earth does that boy have to do with this idiotic scheme?"

"He's not a boy anymore. He's a grown man, and he's coming along, Annette. Didn't we tell you? I've asked Anne Picoté to come with me. Her husband is at Fort Pontchartrain, after all, and she'll be a great help with the boys. It's handy that her brother is of an age to conduct the business part of the venture. And he's promised to conduct it exactly the way that I've planned it out. He'll come along with us for show, though of course he will return to Québec at his earliest convenience. He has no interest in western settlement—at least not at the moment." With that last airy remark, Marie-Thérèse reached for Annette's shawl and tucked it back around her sister-in-law's shoulders. "I'm so sorry, *chérie,* that I won't be able to talk with you longer. Your visits really are a pleasure—but I'm expected in Lower Town. I've a meeting with Pierre Roy, and he prefers not to come up here. He tells me the air is fresher in the taverns than it is this close to the Château, for some reason. I can't imagine why." The sarcasm was utterly lost on her sister-in-law. Marie-Thérèse walked Annette toward the door as they talked, urged her through it, and shut it firmly behind her. She collapsed for a moment against the inside wall. The she looked upward toward the stairwell.

"Anne? Anne! Where are you hiding? She's finally gone," Marie-Thérèse called, straightening up. "The coast is clear!"

"I can hear myself think, so she must be," Anne replied, coming down the stairs. "I swear, Judith is the only one of us who is free from her screeching. You've got a letter from Antoine. It's under the dish on the sideboard. I was afraid Annette would see it and it would start her off again. The messenger brought it this afternoon while you were at the monastery. Will he have heard of your decision to come west, do you think?"

"Not in time to have written me back this quickly." Marie-Thérèse was tearing at the seal as she spoke. "This is a fat one. I hope he has good things to say. We're certainly not turning back now." She scanned the first few lines. "Oh, Anne! Listen!"

"'My dearest wife,'" she read aloud. "'We have completed our fortifications, and I can promise you that Fort Pontchartrain, *Ville du Détroit,* as I see it today, is very much the beginning of the community you and I discussed. You may know that our canoes arrived here on July 23. Getting to *le détroit* took far longer than we had hoped because we chose that northern route—with all those damnable *portages.* But if we added a month to our journey, at least we guaranteed that we would avoid the Iroquois at a time that we were not well equipped to fight them, nor should have fought them. But now, we give almost no thought to the Iroquois threat at all—at least not today, though, of course we may need to do so in future.

"'Thérèse, we've built ourselves a fort that will withstand any sort of raid. It's at the very narrowest point of the river. We have natural water on two sides of us, because we built on top of a bluff at a point where the river *Détroit* and a river we call the Savoyard meet. It's a solid fort. The stockade is made of twenty-foot logs, and they are planted deeply enough to stand for years. Even with the first four feet of each log driven into the ground, there's still a good sixteen feet of wall standing between us and any approaching force. We've put a bastion at each corner of the fort so that we can fire at attackers from three directions at the same time—no matter which wall they attack. I swear to you, I feel like a king in my castle, high on my own hill, absolutely snug and secure.

"'The fort itself is as much a town as fortification. Even the stockade is built with that in mind. We've cut two gates in it—one on the river, and one on the east side near the church of Ste. Anne. Tell your Ursulines that we put up a church right away. We broke ground for it the very first thing, and even managed to have a service there on July 26. They'll have to forgive us for the name; it was the holy Ste. Anne's feast day, so we couldn't exactly call it the church of Ste. Ursula, now could we?

"'We've laid out streets, too. Ste. Anne's is on the main street, with a shorter street paralleling it, and then there are two streets crossing them both, running from north to south. We've marked out lots for dwelling-houses—twenty-five feet by twenty-five feet each. There's a large warehouse, of course. I've allowed myself a little more space for my own house and for Alphonse's headquarters, but for the most part we've kept things small. We need to save room and get as many families inside the fort as possible. It keeps more people safe, and—let us face it, *chérie*—they pay us more rent that way. Later on, *habitants* will build their farms along the river. There they can build as large as they like.

"'And the surrounding country—Thérèse, this is a paradise. The river itself is a channel between lakes—a natural road for further westward exploration. Its banks are rich, grassy meadows dotted with wild orchards—fruit trees so heavily laden that their branches drag on the ground with their own weight. There's every kind of wildlife: deer, game birds—I can't name them all. The local tribes even tell us that this far south the winters are mild. We will soon find out if that is true. I think that perhaps being this close to so much water keeps the temperature from getting as cold as it does in the middle of the forest.

"'I have to admit that all is not perfect here. One of these days I may throttle the good Father Vaillant. More of that in another letter. I have just gone through it all for Count Pontchartrain in Paris, and I've no desire to think of it yet again. But, *mon amour,* you can tuck the boys in tonight and tell them that their father is building a city, and that one day soon, he will come to take them to it.'"

⚜   ⚜   ⚜

"You're determined to do this thing, aren't you? Have you thought of all that could happen?" Pierre Roy's snapping dark eyes didn't twinkle this day. Instead, he looked steadily at Marie-Thérèse, waiting for her answer. When she didn't speak, he went on: "You will be cold. You will be tired. And no one will be able to allow for that. You and Anne and the children will be in the same canoes with the *voyageurs*. What they face, you will face. By the time you begin your journey, it will be late in the year. There'll be no stopping to rest, because of the risk of being trapped by winter. You may travel through hostile territory. There may be days where food must be raw or cold, because building a fire could invite an attack. You know this?"

Marie-Thérèse nodded. "I've thought about it, Monsieur Roy, but I can't get past the fact that it seems the right thing to do. All my children are old enough to travel or have a safe place to wait

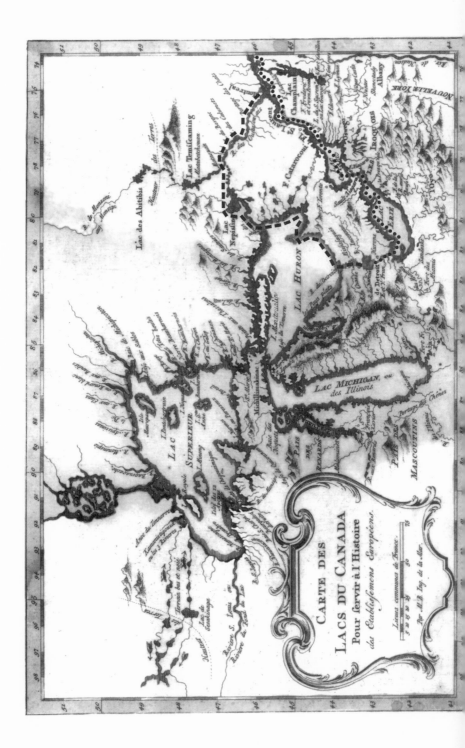

CARTE DES
LACS DU CANADA
Pour servir à l'Histoire
des Etablissemens Européens.

Antoine and Marie-Thérèse's Routes to Fort Pontchartrain, Ville du Détroit. This map—without Antoine and Marie-Therese's routes drawn on it—was made in 1773. Compare it to the 1719 map shown on p. 170–71 of this book. This later map shows the lakes and peninsulas closer to their real shape—although the sizes are still wrong. This is because once Fort Pontchartrain *ville du Détroit* protected the water routes to the west, it became easier to map the lakes more accurately. You'll find many place names that are the same ones that we use today. Best of all, this mapmaker, unlike the man who drew the older map, has put Detroit in the right place!

The broken line from Montreal traces the northern route that Antoine used when he first came to Detroit in July 1701. The round dotted line from Québec (just off the right edge of the map to the east) to *"le Détroit"* represents the southern route Marie-Thérèse took three months later. (M. B. Ing de la Mar, *Carte des Lacs du Canada*, National Archives of Canada, NMC 115817.)

for me. That may not be the case again for years. I have nothing to hold me here. I even have Anne—who is eager to travel with me because her husband is also at Fort Pontchartrain, at Antoine's side. I've thought about the worst that could happen—but I can't close my mind to the best. And, Monsieur Roy—I want to see the new land. I feel—I feel almost trapped, here in Québec."

Pierre Roy nodded—not smiling, but satisfied. "Well then, what's your relationship with the *voyageurs* who will be taking you there?"

Marie-Thérèse launched into an elaborate description of the ends to which she and Anne had gone to persuade François-Marie to intercede for them. The *voyageurs* would cooperate only if they considered the women "passengers"—just that much more freight. They could not and would not take orders from freight. "But they listen to François-Marie because he pays them—and I tell François-Marie what to say."

"Good—good," muttered Pierre Roy, scratching himself and stretching. "You have convinced them all to follow in the footsteps of Antoine Cadillac. Do you think you can convince them to take a different route to *le détroit?*" He leaned forward and spread a map out on the bench between them. "See, here? This is the way your Antoine traveled—here to the north. It's a long, slow difficult trek, and you are hauling your canoes out of the water about every ten

147

miles. Now, look here. One day soon I will go to *le détroit,* and this is the way I will go. This is the old way, and it is a better way." His finger drew a line up the St. Lawrence River toward *Lac Frontenac,* the first of the great waters, and paused. "Some call this *Lac Ontario,*" he said. The finger continued straight across the lake to pick up the river again, where it led from Frontenac to another great water—this one labeled *Lac Érié.* He paused. "Here," he said, "is your only trouble on the southern route—your only *portage*— if you don't decide to avoid the current and go ashore at Point Pélee. But this *portage* is a long one. You'll have six, maybe ten miles that you'll have to carry every single stick you brought with you, and the canoes besides. You and Anne and the children will be expected to walk it, and you may have to carry your share." Marie-Thérèse nodded. This was the route she'd heard Antoine describe so many times. The finger moved to the north shore of *Lac Érié.* "You stay close to the north shore of the lake. It is shorter, and safer, and much further from the English. Here . . ." the finger drew a path northward again. "Here is the river *Détroit*—the river of Antoine Cadillac's straits. And here . . ." he stopped at a spot just before the river widened out into a small lake, "is Fort Pontchartrain."

Marie-Thérèse picked up the map and held it, turning it so that the sunlight shone on it more directly. "It looks so simple. Antoine didn't go this way because de Callières was afraid the Iroquois would 'object,' he said. 'Object,' indeed! The governor talked of nothing short of massacre. Why is it safe now to go this way, just two or three months later?"

"Because, now, the treaty with the Iroquois has been signed. It was being negotiated—sorted out and arranged—right at the time that Antoine left for *le détroit.* Antoine came with soldiers—a good many of them. He was an invading force. I don't think that Governor de Callières cared that much whether or not our Antoine was massacred." Marie-Therese looked up sharply. Pierre Roy shrugged and went on. "The danger was that, had Antoine come through Iroquois territory with what looked like an army, the Iroquois might have refused to sign the treaty. So Antoine must take the northern route. Now, your *voyageurs* are familiar to the Iroquois. They come for beaver, and they go away again. They are no threat. They will not invite attack. And if you and your friend Anne can look like *voyageurs* instead of fine ladies, it's likely you'll draw no attention at all. If you do, well . . ." Pierre Roy shrugged.

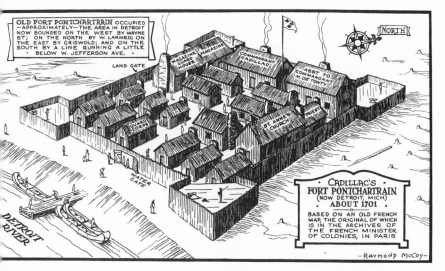

Within the illustration:

OLD FORT PONTCHARTRAIN OCCUPIED —APPROXIMATELY—THE AREA IN DETROIT NOW BOUNDED ON THE WEST BY WAYNE ST; ON THE NORTH BY W. LARNED; ON THE EAST BY GRISWOLD; AND ON THE SOUTH BY A LINE RUNNING A LITTLE · BELOW W. JEFFERSON AVE. ·

NORTH

LAND GATE

MAGAZINE GUARD HOUSE · MAGAZINE · COMMANDANT CADILLAC · ASST. TO COMMANDANT M. DE TONTY

GUARD HOUSE · ST. ANNE'S CHURCH · PRIEST

WATER GATE

DETROIT RIVER

· CADILLAC'S · FORT PONTCHARTRAIN (NOW DETROIT, MICH) · ABOUT 1701 · BASED ON AN OLD FRENCH MAP, THE ORIGINAL OF WHICH IS IN THE ARCHIVES OF THE FRENCH MINISTER OF COLONIES, IN PARIS

—RAYMOND McCOY—

FORT PONTCHARTRAIN. By the time Marie-Thérèse arrived at Fort Pontchartrain, it would have looked much like this. The fort was crowded and busy and was dirtier and a lot smellier than Québec. Its houses were small and close together so that more of them would fit safely inside the walls of the fort. The fort itself was protected by water on three sides. The Savoyard River flowed around and then behind the fort, and the Detroit River ran in front of it. The cliff between the fort and the Detroit River was much higher than it appears in this sketch (see illustration p. 167). The logs used for the buildings in Fort Pontchartrain all stood on end. This kind of construction was called *poteaux en terre* (posts in the ground). It was possible to build faster this way than if the logs were laid lengthwise and crossed at the ends. Poteaux en terre construction used up fewer logs, too. (Raymond McCoy, "Cadillac's Fort Pontchartrain [now Detroit, Mich.] about 1701," in *The Massacre of Fort Mackinaw* [Bay City: private publication, 1956]. Courtesy of the Burton Historical Collection, Detroit Public Library. Photo by Tom Sherry.)

"But if you go this way, you will get to *le détroit* very quickly—long before any threat of winter. You have contracted with Joseph Trottier Desruisseau?" Marie-Thérèse nodded again. "He is a good man. A bit surly, but a good man. He will think ladies still will fear the Iroquois and want the safe northern passage, but he would come this way himself, left to it. If François-Marie suggests it, he will jump at the chance to go by way of the St. Lawrence.

149

"Go on to *le détroit, petite* Madame." Pierre Roy reached out one large hand to touch hers. "I will see you there myself before the next trapping season comes around."

He stood up, and Marie-Thérèse saw that the interview was over. She rose as well, and held out both her hands. "Thank you, Monsieur. Thank you for excellent advice, and thank you more for not telling me to stay here in Québec. I've certainly heard enough of *that* from everyone else!"

Suddenly Pierre Roy was Al-soom-se's merry Uncle Pierre, again. He threw his head back and laughed aloud. "As soon tell the wind to stay here, I think, *non?*" He was still chuckling to himself when Marie-Thérèse made her final farewells and headed back toward Upper Town.

The next day brought a more difficult farewell, for it was August 26, the day that Judith and Madeleine were to move to the monastery. Al-soom-se and Mother Mary of the Angels were there to greet them. Marie-Thérèse swallowed hard, determined not to cry in front of the girls and make them feel worse than they probably did already. She knelt before them and hugged them both to her—hard. They'd done all their talking the night before. Now Judith stepped back and pointed to Marie-Thérèse, then to herself. She turned and hugged her sister quickly, then turned back toward Marie-Thérèse, her small chin set in a determined expression.

"Yes, *chérie*. You will be mother now," Marie-Thérèse nodded vigorously, and watched as Madeleine reached out to grip her sister's hand. "Now, don't you cry. I'll see you again before we leave, and—after that, you are going to be very busy here. You are going to learn to be fine ladies."

"Tell us stories when you come back?" Madeleine asked. "When you come back from the fort?"

"Oh yes—many, many stories when I come back, and before then, too, for we'll not leave yet for a little while. Once I am at Fort Pontchartrain, I'll write all the stories and put them in letters to Mother Mary and Al—and Sister St. Alexis—and they will teach you to read them for yourselves. But you run along now with Sister St. Alexis and get yourselves settled in. I must go home and meet with your uncles."

Al-soom-se took each child by the hand and led them away. Mother Mary and Marie-Thérèse stood watching the little trio as it disappeared into the dormitory building.

Marie-Thérèse blinked and swallowed. "It's hard to imagine all this was burned," she heard Mother Mary say. She knew she was supposed to answer.

"Yes," she gulped. "It's all put back again—better than ever before."

"Just as you will be with your girls again—better than ever before, I think." Mother Mary led the way toward the chapel. "Come, pray with me before you leave." She stopped and looked hard at Marie-Thérèse. "We do not want you to do this thing, you know. All of us here will worry about you. We will not make it more difficult for you by telling you what you should and should not do. You must search your own heart for that. But please know we would keep you here and safe if we could. Since we cannot, I promise you, we will keep your girls safe for you until you return."

Marie-Thérèse could not speak at all. She threw her arms around the elderly nun and hiccuped quietly into her shoulder.

"Come, let us pray," said Mother Mary after a moment, straightening her veil.

⚜ ⚜ ⚜

The following day, Marie-Thérèse was startled to open her front door and find Al-soom-se standing there, a large bundle in her arms, and another in a cart behind her.

"What is it? Has something happened? Is something wrong?" Marie-Thérèse looked about for the girls, but Al-soom-se was alone.

"No, no—nothing like that! The girls are settling in just fine. Judith and I had our first lesson in sign language right after you left. I drew pictures so she could see what the signs meant. When I left just now, she was teaching Madeleine the same signs, using my sketches. The girls will be fine—better than fine.

"No, I've brought you something. Where's Anne?"

"Here I am," called Anne, coming in from the back garden with an armload of fresh greens. "What is this? What do you have?"

Al-soom-se was untying a string that held her bundle, and now she unrolled its contents on the parlor floor. Piece after piece of soft deerskin unfolded before them. It took Marie-Thérèse and Anne a moment to realize they were looking at clothing—fringed and beaded and strange in cut, but clothing nevertheless.

"Uncle Pierre came to the monastery yesterday," Al-soom-se

151

explained. "If you think you were startled to see me this morning, imagine how I felt when I was called to the monastery gate and saw Pierre Roy near that place!

"He said we needed to make you look like *voyageurs* for your trip, but I told him it would be easier to make you look like the Abenaki—and more comfortable for you, I think. The woolens of the *voyageurs* can be brightly colored and beautiful, but they still are stiff and scratchy. Deerskin is soft and warm—and it wears forever.

"Some of these are mine, and some belong to girls at the monastery, but they will be yours for the journey." She held out leggings and small, fringed skirts to wear over them. "Until it's very cold, the Abenaki women wear nothing else, but you, I think, will want to have something on top," she giggled.

Marie-Thérèse felt herself blush.

"I should think so!" Anne said indignantly.

The "something on top" turned out to be deerskin shirts, carefully decorated with tiny beads—trade goods—and something else, something shiny and narrow and flat.

"Ohhhh," breathed Marie-Thérèse. "Porcupine quills! I love quillwork, and I've never seen any that was finer than this. It's so pretty." She ran her fingers across the slick quills, admiring the way they were dyed and sewed firmly into elaborate patterns.

The second bundle held furs stitched together to make warm robes—and several pairs of moccasins. "You'll probably not wear out more than one pair during your trip, but just in case, you'll have extras." Al-soom-se rocked back on her heels and looked up at her friends.

"I don't know how to start thanking you," said Marie-Thérèse. I've been making shirts and trousers for the boys— miniature *voyageur* costumes—but I really wasn't sure what we were going to do for ourselves."

"Thank me by having our adventure for me." Al-soom-se rose to her feet, a dignified Ursuline sister again. Then her eyes twinkled. "Uncle Pierre says he's sent you by way of the great falls. You and my brother—you'll both have seen them. You don't know how I envy you!" She waved gaily, and was out the front door, leaving Marie-Thérèse and Anne to gather up the bundles of deerskin clothing.

"Well—what are we waiting for?" Marie-Thérèse asked. "Let's go upstairs and figure how to put these on!"

❧ 20 ❧
The Southern Route

Marie-Thérèse rubbed her arms and shivered. The September morning was warm, but a chill ran through her body. Québec was behind them now. She was well and truly off on her own, leading her family and her best friend straight into the wilderness. Not for the first time, she doubted everything. Should she be doing this at all? Did she have the right to take others into this much danger? But the answers came as quickly as the questions did. There was nothing else to do. This must be right. There was a pattern. This was the way things were supposed to be. "But what if I am wrong?" she asked herself again.

She sat near the stern of the huge canoe, her back against her bag of clothing. One bag or chest per *voyageur,* one bag per passenger—that was the rule. It had been hard deciding what to take and what to leave. Antoine would expect her to dress well at Fort Pontchartrain—at *le détroit*—so some things had been left out of the boys' bags and replaced with ribbons and fine laces. "Détroit"—she must start thinking of it that way. The *voyageurs* chattered on about the river *Détroit*, the fort at Détroit, and so on. No more just *"le détroit"* as a description of the narrows in the river. Now it was the name of a place. "Well, Antoine, you've at least made sure the word stays on the map," she chuckled to herself. Then she shivered again.

The departure from Québec should have been a gala one. It was not. Both Michel and Jacques were full of last-minute arguments against the trip and against the southern route. Michel stomped off in a huff. Jacques stood near the pier, looking uncomfortable. Annette did not come to see them off at all, but Claudette was there, red-eyed, somehow sure that it was her fault that

Madame Cadillac was leaving Québec. Al-soom-se had brought the girls to say good-bye, and Marie-Thérèse warmed a little as she thought of her daughters standing there, proud and dry-eyed. There was more than a little of the adventurer in both of them—but not enough to see them through the hazards of a trip like the voyage to Détroit. They were better staying there at the monastery with Al-soom-se. What would she have done without Al-soom-se? Uncle François had been at the waterfront this morning—disapproving, but using the chance to send letters to Antoine about some business they were doing somewhere. Uncle François's scowling face would have been her last glimpse of Québec, had she not turned around at just the right moment to see the girls trudging their way back up to Upper Town. She waved and they waved, and then they hurried on. They had to get back to the monastery in time for mass. Mother Mary had asked the Jesuits to say a special mass for Marie-Thérèse's journey.

Ahead of Marie-Thérèse near the stern of the other canoe, she could see Anne and her brother. It looked as if François-Marie was paddling. He probably had been given a paddle because Anne had only Monsieur Trottier with her as steersman and guide. With Marie-Thérèse were two burly *Canadiens*, Toussaint Pothier dit Laverdure and Robert Réaume, there to guide her canoe. Both canoes were heavy—piled high with trade goods. She watched the muscles in the backs of the Abenaki paddlers ripple as they bent and pushed and lifted, bent and pushed and lifted, driving the canoes over the water. Each man turned his paddle slightly as it broke the surface, so there was no splash. Except for the sound of the river itself, their passage was silent. Even the boys were quiet, staring as the shoreline as it slipped by. Once Joseph nudged his brother and pointed. Marie-Thérèse looked to see what had caught their attention. At the water's edge, a doe and two half-grown fawns were drinking. Where was the buck? Behind them, nearer the forest, she saw him. Even at this distance, she could count one-two-three-four points on each antler. An eight-point buck—a big one. As she watched, he and his family slipped back into the forest.

The days sped by. At first they were blessed with good weather. Maybe Mother Mary's mass had something to do with that, Marie-Thérèse thought. It seemed strange not to chatter with Anne. At first they called back and forth to each other, but Monsieur

Trottier stopped them. "You want the whole Iroquois nation to know I'm saddled with two helpless women?" he growled. After that, Marie-Thérèse and Anne were quiet and saved their comments to share at night when they camped.

Marie-Thérèse tried playing word games with the boys to keep them entertained, but after a while found that it was better to leave them to their own devices. Eleven years old and six years old—so young for such a trip! But they quickly made friends with the Abenaki braves. One evening after the party had made camp for the night, they rushed up to Marie-Thérèse.

"Look, Mama!" cried Jacques, holding out his prize. Each boy had a small paddle, cut hastily from driftwood and roughly shaped with a knife.

"We have to scrape them until they are smooth. But when they are smooth enough, we can use them to help paddle the canoe!"

"How do I thank the Abenaki, Monsieur Réaume?" Marie-Thérèse asked. "Someone must have done without sleep to make those."

"They'd not want your thanks, Madame," he replied—only slightly more pleasantly than Monsieur Trottier would have spoken. Taking women and children into the forest was not his idea of the life of a *voyageur.*

After that, the boys worked to learn to paddle as silently as the Abenaki. Their small forms bent and pushed and lifted in rhythm with the other paddlers. Marie-Thérèse envied them. Tired of just sitting, she borrowed his paddle from an impatient Joseph and practiced, careful to keep in step with the others. The next morning when she awoke, two full size paddles lay next to her—spares, pulled from the stores they carried. She gave one to Anne. They found that they didn't have the strength to paddle for long periods, but doing so for a little while at a time broke up the day.

Surprisingly soon the canoes reached the place where the river met *Lac Frontenac*—the first of the great waters, the one Pierre Roy had said sometimes was called "Ontario." Marie-Thérèse caught herself looking toward the shore, seeking an abandoned canoe pulled up into the reeds and waiting there for Al-soom-se's brother. She looked ahead and saw Anne scanning the same shoreline. Anne caught her eye and grinned. They had been thinking about the same thing.

Days stretched into weeks. It was chillier at night now, but there had been only one really hard rain. Marie-Thérèse and Anne put the boys between them and huddled under a blanket stretched overhead to give them shelter. The blanket kept off the raindrops that came straight down, but most of the rain blew from side to side. It was days before they felt as if they had dried out, and then, of course, it rained again.

They paddled across the vastness that was *Lac Frontenac* and came to the river leading upstream to *Lac Érié*. Marie-Thérèse remembered Al-soom-se's brother again. "For a while he could paddle along easily, but then the water moved faster and faster toward him and turned white with its speed," she whispered to herself. That night, Monsieur Trottier talked to his passengers about the upcoming *portage*.

"You will carry your own packs, *Mesdames*—your own bags. You will carry the paddles that you are using. The *voyageurs* and the Abenaki will carry the rest. If you are tired, do not stop. Keep up. The Iroquois are more apt to attack those who fall behind than they are to take on the whole party—so we must not have stragglers. We are on the south shore of the river because the walking is easier here, but we must remember that the south shore belongs to the Iroquois." He turned on his heel and walked abruptly back to the campfire.

Anne looked decidedly uneasy.

"He built a fire tonight. He can't be too much afraid of the Iroquois," comforted Marie-Thérèse, "and we do have the treaty, now."

The night, as it turned out, was quiet, but the *portage* the next day was horrible—at least from Marie-Thérèse's and Anne's points of view. The *voyageurs* and Abenaki seemed to take it all in stride. The canoes were drawn ashore and unloaded and the trade goods and other bundles carried by hand. The canoes themselves were hoisted to the shoulders of the strongest men, and the party set out. Marie-Thérèse guessed that she and Anne were carrying no more than fifty or seventy-five pounds each, but the way her back and shoulders ached, it might as well have been a ton. When she stumbled and fell, which she did frequently, it felt as if the pack on her back was pushing her into the ground. Some of the men carried twice as much weight as she—well over a hundred pounds each. Still, some of the goods had to be left behind in a cache, piled up and hidden carefully.

Men from the party then must return to get it and carry it back along the path to the point where the canoes could be put in the river again. In all, nearly ten miles had to be crossed on land— sometimes more than once—and they could move only a few hard miles each day.

There was a clear trail—and there was the river to follow as well. But at every step, there was the danger that the Iroquois could have broken the treaty and be waiting around the next bend, the next patch of trees. To avoid hunting parties, the *voyageurs* kept them as close to the river as they dared, but this forced them to walk where the ground was roughest. Even the *voyageurs* were exhausted. Breath was short, and tempers were shorter.

One night, their camp was not far from the great falls. Tired as she was, Marie-Thérèse made herself walk to the river's edge to look upward at the wall of water that faced Al-soom-se's brother those many years before. The noise surrounding her was incredible. The air was so filled with mist that in minutes her hair was soaked and her deerskin shirt turned brown with damp. She tried to imagine getting close enough to the falls to hide behind them. She shook her head in wonder. "Not tonight, at least," she thought. "One drop of water would knock me off balance. I'm that tired."

She was still sitting there, arms wrapped around her knees, gazing at the water, when Anne found her.

"Hurry! Hurry! Come back to the camp! Something's happened—I don't know what. They've pulled everybody together, and it's all very, very quiet." Anne's face was white in the darkness, and her voice was tense.

Back with the others, the two women were greeted by a scene of quiet confusion. Toussaint Pothier seemed to be arguing that they pack up camp and move on, even though it was night. Monsieur Trottier was just as determined that they stay, but it sounded as if he was talking about withdrawing into the forest. "What is it? What's going on?" asked Marie-Thérèse, of anyone who would listen.

Robert Réaume answered her. "Our scouts have spotted a party of Iroquois just upriver from us."

"A war party?" gasped Anne.

"It seems not. They aren't wearing paint, and they have a black-robe with them."

"A prisoner?" asked Marie-Thérèse.

"No. He seems to be part of the party. That is why Joseph Trottier feels we are safe here, as long as we take reasonable care. We . . ." he broke off.

At the edge of the clearing he had spotted a tall, black-robed figure. The man stood alone, but he was obviously the priest who had been seen with the Iroquois. Anne and Marie-Thérèse were quick to join the group that pressed forward to greet the newcomer. The priest calmly examined the Abenaki and *voyageurs* hurrying toward him, and, after a moment, decided on Joseph Trottier as a likely authority.

"Is all well here?" he demanded of Trottier. "My friends told me that there was a party of Abenaki and *voyageurs* coming toward us on the trail. They said you had women among you. Were these women captives? Have you ransomed them? Are they in need of religious counsel?"

Since Marie-Thérèse was standing directly under the priest's nose, she saw no reason why he should speak of her in the third person. She cut in before Joseph Trottier could reply. "I am Marie-Thérèse Lamothe Cadillac," she said. "I am on my way to be with my husband at Fort Pontchartrain. This is my friend Anne de Tonty. Her husband likewise is at Fort Pontchartrain. We have no need of religious counsel, but we thank you for your concern. And who are you, please, Father?"

The priest stepped back, as startled as he would have been had one of the forest animals spoken to him. "Madame Cadillac?" he said in wonder. "Madame, I am Father François Vaillant de Gueslis. I have come from Fort Pontchartrain, where I had the honor to work with your husband. But I wonder that he has permitted you to travel this wilderness. Surely you would have been better to stay at home with your family!" He shook his head, as if to clear his thinking. "Were I your family's priest, I certainly would have forbidden you to do such at thing. The danger here is quite intense, and the living at Fort Pontchartrain totally unfit for females—and will be until another year has passed."

Marie-Thérèse bristled at the thought of this man—or any strange man—thinking that he had the right to "forbid" her to do anything. Yet Father Vaillant's distress was obvious. He wasn't just telling her to stay home because she was a woman. He really was afraid for her and for Anne.

"Don't waste pity on us," Marie-Thérèse said. *"When a woman loves her husband, no place where he is can be dangerous."*

Father Vaillant pressed his lips together tightly. He spoke as though his teeth were clenched. "You are misguided, Madame, but you are here. We will pray for your safe journey." He turned to Joseph Trottier. "My camp is close by. You will pass it on tomorrow's portage. You and Madame Cadillac and Madame de Tonty and all of your party who are Christian will hear mass with us in the morning." He turned and stalked back into the forest the way he had come.

"So that is Father Vaillant," said Marie-Thérèse to Anne. "No wonder Antoine wants to throttle him!"

"He's a hard man, but I think he's a good one," replied Anne.

"And a stubborn one, I'll bet," replied Marie-Thérèse. "His kind disagree with Antoine on almost everything. I don't imagine the good Father Vaillant is willing to change his mind very often."

Bone-weary, they ate cold food (the fire had been doused as soon as the Iroquois camp was spotted) and rolled up in their blankets to sleep. Marie-Thérèse was glad of the promise of mass in the morning, though she knew that the lost time would make Monsieur Trottier push them harder along the trail. It would be her first close look at the Iroquois, too. She couldn't decide whether that made her feel afraid or excited. "I guess I'll find out in the morning," she thought, and rolled over and went to sleep.

Father Vaillant's camp included a chapel among the rocks near the river. Afterwards, Marie-Thérèse thought of that little church service as one of the highlights of her journey. The birds overhead sang loudly; the rush of the falls played constantly in the background. And throughout the mass, she was conscious of Iroquois eyes watching her. The Iroquois seemed fascinated to have two white women among them. Several even came up to her and kissed her hands in greeting in the French fashion. She held her breath to keep from pulling away and insulting them. They smelled of the mixture of rancid bear fat and skunk oil that was smeared on their bodies. "Bear grease" protected the Iroquois from strong winds and cold and chapped skin. In the summer it prevented sunburn and kept away insects. Summer or winter, it smelled bad—not at all like the fine bear oil Marie-Thérèse used for cooking. She made herself smile at them. Out of the corner of her eye, she saw that Anne also was managing to stand her ground, but the tight expression on her face showed that her

Iroquois, too, had protected themselves against the chilly nights by smearing themselves with the smelly fat.

The remaining days of the *portage* were uneventful. "For that matter, what else could happen to us?" Marie-Thérèse asked Anne. "I mean, beyond running into a real war party." They were back in the canoes, well across *Lac Érié*, before she had an answer.

Once again, the weather was beautiful. It was October now, and each morning when the sun hit the trees, it filled the world with more and more color. First just smudges of red showed at the top of green trees. Then, a few days later, whole trees burst

THE END OF A PORTAGE. If a section of river was full of rocks and rapids, travelers were forced to make a *portage*. Days or weeks before the time of this picture, these people pulled their canoes out of the river, unloaded them, and began to haul everything overland. Bundles that couldn't be carried in the first trip were stored in a safe place, or *cache*. Once the travelers reached the end of a *portage*, they set up camp and sent some of their party back for goods left behind. Here, the first canoe to complete the *portage* is being used as a shelter. Notice how the men carrying things are bent over? Each man not helping to carry a canoe carried a hundred pounds or more of goods on his back. (William Armstrong, *Indians Completing a Portage*, National Archives of Canada, C-019041.)

forth in bright golds and oranges. Rows of low, scrubby sumac made up for their small size with the brightness of their red leaves. Behind them, maples were bold in pinkish orange and lighter red. The pale yellow of birch and poplar turned silver as wind passed over the leaves. Even the oaks were golden, though occasionally Marie-Thérèse saw oak trees that were a darker, dusty red. Sometimes the canoes passed low, flat land covered with seemingly endless stands of dark, dark pine trees. Then the land would change, and color burst forth again.

"I don't remember seeing a fall like this, do you?" asked Anne, and then started to answer herself, "except . . ."

"Yes—except the year of the fire." Marie-Thérèse was quiet a moment. For a change, she and Anne were in the same canoe. As the boys became more accustomed to traveling, it was easy to leave them under the general supervision of François-Marie Picoté. The boys liked being in the "men's canoe," and the time went far faster when Anne and Marie-Thérèse could talk about the things they were seeing.

"Hey! Hey!" there was a flurry of shouting up ahead.

"What in the world?" Marie-Thérèse leaned forward in alarm.

"It's all right," said Anne. "It's not François-Marie's canoe. It's the little one."

Although they began the trip in Québec with two large canoes, while they were still in *Lac Frontenac* they had been joined by a third, smaller one. In it were four men, one of whom was quite young and—surprisingly—English. Because it was so much safer to travel in large groups, the extra canoe was a welcome addition to the party. The new men kept much to themselves, and, except for occasional failing attempts to talk to the English boy, Marie-Thérèse paid little attention to the extra canoe or the people in it.

Now the three men were paddling back toward them, shouting as they came. Marie-Thérèse couldn't see the boy at first. Then she spotted him lying back against the canoe's load of supplies. When they were even with Monsieur Trottier's canoe, Trottier reached out a hand and pulled the two canoes together. The shouting died down, but Marie-Thérèse could see that everyone still was talking excitedly. The boy hadn't moved.

Monsieur Trottier let go of the little canoe and stood up in the stern of the larger one. He waved his arm at them and then pointed to the land. He waited to be certain they understood and then sat down to steer as the two canoes, large and small, raced for the shore.

Once ashore, Monsieur Trottier called them all together.

"I have to stay here," he announced. "The boy will die without me. He is badly hurt. He cannot travel. I am as good as a doctor. I stay here."

Everyone started shouting at once. Marie-Thérèse stole a glance at the boy. He still hadn't moved. He didn't look too sick, but he held one arm stiffly across his chest. "Perhaps I can help," she spoke up. "I have worked in the Hôtel Dieu."

"You? No, Madame! That will not be at all necessary." Monsieur Trottier spoke hurriedly. "No. It is settled. I will stay."

"But what happened to him?" Marie-Thérèse asked, pointing to the boy.

One of the men from the little canoe stepped forward to answer her. "It was a freak accident, Madame. He is badly wounded. We were hunting. We intended to catch up with you tonight and bring meat. He shot a deer, and went up to it to dress it. Only it was not dead, and it charged him. He took an antler through his shoulder and another prong went through his arm. It's good that it happened here, if it had to happen at all. We have camped here before. There is a small shelter already built. Monsieur Trottier is good with wounds. He will stay with us here until the boy is well."

"For how long will that be?" asked Marie-Thérèse.

"Possibly until spring. You go back to your own children now. Monsieur Trottier has seen to it that you have someone to take you on to Détroit."

Marie-Thérèse looked back at the canoe that had been Anne's and Monsieur Trottier's. Sitting in the stern to steer it, she saw a tall Abenaki brave. Anne followed her glance. "He knows the way," she whispered. "That's the one who made the paddles for the boys. He's been to Détroit before."

Joseph Trottier stood on the shore, a locked chest at his feet. "Come on, Marie-Thérèse," urged Anne. "Everyone else is on board the canoes."

Marie-Thérèse let herself be led back to her canoe. As she settled down in her usual spot, she turned back to Anne. "How did Monsieur Trottier get his bundles out of the canoe so quickly? There's something funny about this. That boy didn't look that much hurt to me, and I've treated wounds before. And they had a camp right there? Waiting for them? There's something not right."

"Well, I'm not going to worry about it," said Anne firmly. "And neither should you. What we need to worry about is getting to Fort Pontchartrain while this weather holds."

Marie-Thérèse continued to puzzle to herself, but it would be nearly a year before she knew the rest of the story. The following August, Joseph Trottier would be brought to trial in Montreal for stealing from Anne's canoe and trading stolen goods for beaver pelts—something that was doubly illegal because the beaver trade now belonged to Fort Pontchartrain. Trottier apparently did his illegal trading during the winter that he spent at Long Point (the location of his *Lac Érié* camp) nursing the English boy back to health. Marie-Thérèse heard the news the following Christmas. "I knew it! I knew it!" she crowed to Antoine. "They made it all up. It was planned. They waited until they got to the spot where they already had a camp, the boy pretended to get hurt, and Monsieur Trottier was all ready to leave our party with some of our trade goods! I told Anne there was something funny going on."

But that would be more than a year from now. For now, all Marie-Thérèse could do was look back toward the little group of men on the shore and wonder. . . .

❖ 21 ❖
Fort Pontchartrain, Ville du Détroit

The days were routine now: break camp in the morning, pile aboard the canoes, paddle a little, rest a little and smoke a pipe, then paddle some more. The *voyageurs* actually measured each day's travel by how many pipes they smoked. Marie-Thérèse watched as the Abenaki wielded their canoe paddles. The Abenaki never rested. They rarely paused. Occasionally they ran a canoe ashore to hunt. Progress was steady. The weather remained clear and warm, and the autumn colors increased their brilliance.

At long last came the morning that François-Marie Picoté strolled to the women's end of the camp. *"Bonjour, Mesdames!"* he called gaily. "I've been talking to Robert Réaume. I think you may not want to wear your deerskins today!"

Anne and Marie-Thérèse caught their breaths. They knew what he meant, but Marie-Thérèse still had to hear the words. "It will be today? You mean we'll get there today?"

"Before midday, they say. Dress your best," he said laughing.

Anne and Marie-Thérèse looked at each other. After a little over a month on the trail, they were not as easy to recognize as white women as they had been. Their hair was braided to keep it out of their way. Their faces were windburned. Their deerskins were soiled. Even their spare moccasins were beginning to show wear. But they had known this day would come when they began the trip, and they were prepared. Anne went back to the canoe and gave some instructions. Soon a chest was brought to them. Marie-Thérèse opened it. Inside were the brightest colored gowns they owned. The Iroquois liked bright colors, Antoine had told them once, long ago. So, for that matter, did the Abenaki, at home in Québec. There would be many tribes at Fort Pontchartrain: Ottawa, Potawatomi, Ojibwa—the Huron, too. They were really in the land of the Huron! She smiled to herself, thinking of Al-soom-se's brother, and turned back to the open chest in front of her. Marie-Thérèse and Anne would dress to please their husbands, but they also would dress to please the men who were such an important part of the fur trade.

It hardly seemed real to put on the stiff petticoats and fine

THE ARRIVAL OF MADAME CADILLAC. In 1901, when Detroit was celebrating the 200th anniversary of its founding, a sculptor named Carlos Romanelli created this bronze plaque. In it, warriors at the left have dropped their bows and arrows to show that Marie-Thérèse's arrival begins a time of peace. Marie-Thérèse is just about to step ashore while Antoine holds out his arm to keep her from tripping. Either Joseph or Jacques is standing next to Marie-Thérèse, waiting for his turn to jump out of the canoe. Led by Alphonse Tonty, all the soldiers from the fort have crowded together on the riverfront, and one man holds his sword high in salute. The photographer who took this picture has made the plaque into an even better work of art by using light in a special way. It looks as if the sun will shine on Marie-Thérèse at the very moment she steps out of the canoe. (Carlos Romanelli, *The Arrival of Mme Cadillac*, Cadillac Station, Detroit People Mover, Detroit, Mich. Photo by Balthasar Korab.)

laces of a French gentlewoman again. They washed as best they could in the shallows of the lake. "If I put my hair up, it won't matter that it's greasy. It's too late in the year to wash it properly in any case," said Marie-Thérèse. "But can you help me with this *frontage?*" Stiffly starched lace stood up over her forehead just as it should, but she was so excited her fingers wouldn't work to tie its strings.

Anne's fingers flew as she knotted the laces of the *frontage.* "I brought perfume, if you did not." She nodded toward her own opened bundle. "We smell like warriors greased for winter."

Finally they were ready. "I guess that's the best we can do," said Anne. "You look wonderful. How about me?"

"You do, too," said Marie-Thérèse. "Honestly, my heart is pounding faster than it did when we thought the Iroquois were going to attack us at the falls."

They heard François-Marie call. "Where are the boys?" asked Anne.

Marie-Thérèse looked around them. "I'm not sure. François-Marie said he would see that they cleaned up properly."

"Right here, Mama." Joseph appeared before them, still dressed like a *voyageur,* but with a clean shirt and a bright sash around his waist. Small Jacques's sash was so long it dragged on the ground, but otherwise he was as clean and neat as his brother.

Once aboard the canoe, Marie-Thérèse found to her dismay that she couldn't use her paddle because the sleeves of her dress were so tight. "What a day to just *sit* here!" she fumed. "I can't stand doing *nothing.*"

They were no longer in the lake, but were moving steadily up a wide river. The sun was almost overhead when the waters began to narrow. "BOOM!" A noise louder than thunder broke the air.

Anne shrieked. Marie-Thérèse jumped a little. "It's cannon, Mama!" yelled Joseph. "It's cannon! They know we are coming!"

When they came around the next bend in the river, they could see the fort ahead of them to their left. As they watched, a puff of smoke appeared by one of the bastions. "BOOM!" the cannon roared out again.

Now they were close enough to see a crowd of people gathered between a gate in the side of the fort and the river. A small pier extended out over the water, and part of the group made its way to stand on it.

THE FIRST LADY OF DETROIT, OCTOBER 1701. Robert Thom's *Mme Cadillac Arrives in Detroit* captures all the hustle and bustle of the moment when Marie-Thérèse Guyon becomes the First Lady of Detroit. In the center of the picture, Antoine welcomes Marie-Thérèse to Fort Pontchartrain. To their right, Joseph, still dressed like a *voyageur,* is getting ready to swing his brother *petit* Antoine around in a circle. On the left, Alphonse Tonty and a *voyageur* are helping Anne Picoté scramble up onto the dock while another *voyageur* holds onto a pier to steady the canoe. (It's probably wobbling a lot as Anne climbs out and boxes and bales are unloaded.) The *voyageur* holding the pier is well dressed, so he may be Anne's brother, François Picoté de Belestre. In the background, supplies from the arriving canoes are being carried to the fort. You can just see a native encampment, either Algonquian or Iroquoian, on top of the cliff at the far right. Warriors from the camp are firing muskets in celebration. It's all part of the excitement as Detroit greets its own very first lady. (Robert Thom, *Mme Cadillac Arrives in Detroit.* Reproduced courtesy of Ameritech. Print photographed by Irving Berg.)

167

"There's *petit* Antoine! I see *petit* Antoine!" shrieked Jacques.

"Sit down, young man!" hissed Marie-Thérèse. "Before you fall in! I am not bringing you to your father's side dripping wet."

For there was *her* Antoine . . . dressed in the same brilliant yellow brocade and fine lace he'd worn the first time she'd seen him in front of Michel's fire. The canoe bumped up against the pier, and she found herself climbing partly out of it. She reached to pull herself up, only to be caught by strong arms and set on her feet at one end of the pier. Now she had only to walk a few steps and she would reach Antoine—but she discovered that her feet wouldn't move. Out of the corner of one eye, she saw Anne and Alphonse de Tonty locked in an embrace. Beyond them, Joseph and Jacques and *petit* Antoine spun each other around in crazy circles.

The dress she had chosen to wear was a bright crimson silk. Sure enough, Iroquois hands reached out and caught at her skirt. She was just barely aware as other tribesmen crowded around her to touch its brilliance and feel and smell the soft folds. Later she would realize that many nations were there to greet her. Antoine's plan to gather all the tribes into a fur-trading center was well underway.

"They never saw color that bright before in a fabric," smiled Antoine. "You chose well."

Marie-Thérèse still could not move—much less speak. She stood there, numbly. Antoine reached out and took her hand in both of his own. "Welcome to Fort Pontchartrain, Thérèse," he said, smiling. "Welcome to the first lady of Détroit."

The old lady finished speaking and sat back in her chair with a sigh. The sun was nearly gone now, but in the fading light she still could see the upturned faces of the children sitting at her feet.

"Tell us about the time you rescued Governor Cadillac from prison—from the Bastille," said René, but not very loudly. He too was tired.

"Hush, René!" one of the Carmelite nuns stood before them all. "You children run along home. Madame must rest now. Come back tomorrow. She'll tell you then. That is a story for another day."

HISTORICAL NOTES

Before the Story Begins

Most of this story is absolutely true. Of course, we don't know exactly what people said to each other in 1686, and it's impossible to tell everything each person did each day. But we do know a lot about the French settlement in Québec and the way people lived in the seventeenth century. Marie-Thérèse witnessed a lot of history that is documented—that is, written down at the time that it happened. So you see, we can make some very good guesses about what Marie-Thérèse and her friends were doing during the time this story takes place. You can use this and the following pages to tell which events are real and which were made up to show you what life was like in those days.

⚜   ⚜   ⚜

MAP OF NOUVELLE FRANCE. The 1719 map found on the following pages shows *Nouvelle France* the way Antoine and Marie-Thérèse probably thought it looked. Without planes to take photographs, the map was made according to surveyors' calculations—and sometimes by just guessing. In spite of this, it is easy to tell that this is a picture of Michigan and the Great Lakes, though some places have different names than they do today. To help travelers know what lands are safe to cross, the mapmaker has listed the names of local tribes. He's done one important thing wrong, though. He wants to show that *"Fort du Détroit"* guards the water route west, but he's put the fort at the wrong end of the Detroit River! (Henri Abraham Chatelain, *Carte de la Nouvelle France* [Amsterdam, 1719]. Courtesy of the Burton Historical Collection, Detroit Public Library. Photograph by Tom Sherry.)

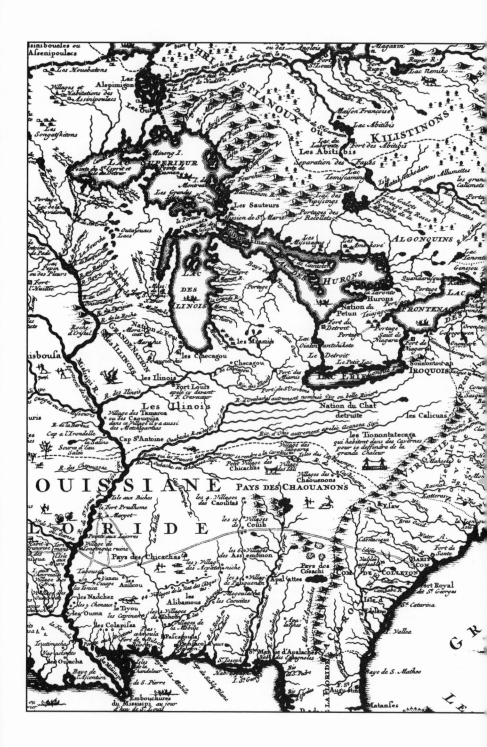

Little is known of Marie-Thérèse Guyon's early childhood, except that she was born in Beauport, not far from Québec. Her father was Denis Guyon, a merchant-farmer, sometimes identified as a master stonemason. Her mother, Elisabeth Boucher, was related to the Duc de Lauzon (Duke of Lauzon) and through him to the French royal family. Her father—and probably her mother also—died sometime between 1684 and 1687. We do not know whether they died from accident or disease, or just because most people in the 1600s did not live much past middle age. Michel Denis and Jacques Guyon, her brothers, may have been her guardians. Their names appear as witness to her marriage in 1687. Her uncle, François Guyon, also plays a part in her story.

Chapter 1

According to the records of the Ursuline Monastery in Québec, Marie-Thérèse Guyon was a boarding student there from March 8, 1683 until April 4, 1684. She returned to the school to live in November of 1685, possibly at the death of one or both of her parents. At that time, she would have been fourteen years old—an age at which most of her friends would have been betrothed or married.

Her lifelong friend Anne Picoté de Belestre is said also to have attended the school, but, as "Anne" seems to have been a nickname, it's hard to tell exactly when she was there. Two different girls with exactly the same name (Anne Picoté de Belestre) boarded at the monastery many years after Marie-Thérèse was there: in 1731 and again, much later, in 1752. The first girl probably was "our" Anne's niece, or possibly a granddaughter. The second definitely was her niece. Records show that the Anne who boarded at the monastery in 1752 was the daughter of François-Marie Picoté de Belestre, Anne's brother, and his second wife. This is interesting, but all it really tells us is that the Picoté de Belestre family liked the school and sent their children there over the years. So for the purposes of this book, I've simply said that Marie-Thérèse and Anne were there at exactly the same time. It could have been true.

Al-soom-se is not "real," but she is what we call a composite character—a combination of other characters that are real. Many daughters of influential Algonquin, Abenaki, and Huron tribesmen and chiefs attended the Ursuline school, and Al-soom-se represents them all. Her Christian name, Denise, is borrowed from a real Abenaki student who attended the school at about the same time that Marie-Thérèse did. Her Abenaki name, Al-soom-se, is a word found in Algonquian languages meaning "independent woman." Western Algonquians (those in tribes living west of the Appalachian and Adirondack mountains) used "Al-soom-se" frequently as a name. Why were there so many native children at the school? The Ursulines taught the Algonquin, Abenaki, and Huron children hoping they would return to their villages and spread the way of life that they had learned at the monastery.

Some students, whether they were French or native, attended the school for as long as six or eight years. Others were there only for twelve short months. All were taught reading, writing, arithmetic, and Christian doctrine and ethics. Because girls were supposed to graduate knowing "all that is most essential in the education of females," they also learned needlework and embroidery, painting, and art appreciation. Since many of the nuns had professed (joined the order) when they were in their twenties and thirties, there were plenty of teachers who could play instruments and train pupils in the latest court dances and the "Language of the Fan" (a fashionable way to communicate by holding and moving a fan in certain ways). So that they could teach all their students equally well, the nuns learned several native languages, including Algonquin and Iroquois. Marie de l'Incarnation herself had learned *both* Iroquois and Algonquin. This was very unusual. One difficult new language usually was all one person could master.

One other thing in this chapter is very real. The ash tree, old in Marie-Thérèse's day, survived the fires and shaded the monastery grounds for over two hundred years. It lost a main branch in 1839 but continued to stand tall. It finally was destroyed in a thunderstorm in August 1868.

You may be wondering why the Ursulines called their church, home, and school a monastery *(monastère)* instead of a convent *(couvent)*. This may have happened because the Ursulines were very active in the community and thought the masculine term better described their life style. When they moved into Madame de la Peltrie's house after the burning of the second monastery, they called the *house* "The Convent of the Ursulines"—a place where they did nothing but live until they could build a new monastery.

Chapter 2

The descriptions given here of Québec's Upper Town and Lower Town are accurate. Of course, we have no idea whether Marie-Thérèse ever led an expedition to the rough and dangerous waterfront, but we certainly know she would have been punished if she had done so—and what sort of punishment it could have been.

Lay sisters, who served the monastery but did not become full-fledged nuns, often were assigned the heaviest and most difficult jobs. Sister Cécile really was one of the lay sisters, but we don't know exactly what kind of work she did. Since the Ursulines believed in moving people from one area of responsibility to another, probably she did many different things.

The sad story of little Agnes Wesk-wes is completely true. Having become used to French and Christian ways, after she graduated from school and was sent home Agnes was desperately unhappy. She begged to be sent back to the monastery. She was allowed to go back to Québec, but, once there, she immediately developed a fever. When it looked as if she was too sick to live, her parents were sent for. They arrived just after Agnes had died. She lay on a bier, her body covered with spring flowers picked by the grieving nuns.

Chapter 3

There is a complete description of the 1686 fire in *Glimpses of the Monastery,* written two hundred years later in 1875. Because it was so important, stories of the burning of the monastery were recorded in great detail right after the fire. Thus we know the exact moment in the mass that the alarm was raised. We know that Mother Superior went to check on the reason for the alarm and just what she said when she came back. (You'll find that her words are written in *italics* in the story. This is your clue that the words are exact. I've used italics for direct quotations—what people really said—and for words that are written in a foreign language, either Latin or French. In this "Historical Notes" section, you'll also find book titles written in italics.) Most astonishingly, *Glimpses* tells us the story of Sister Cécile, left behind in the church during the frantic attempt to save the altar furnishings. It's absolutely true that Sister Cécile had been helping to carry the reliquary, and that she was cut off by fire and escaped by an attic window. There's no record of how she managed to get from the roof to the ground. I've described one way it could have been done. We know that she was all right after the fire (as a matter of fact, she lived to be eighty-one), so it's unlikely that she jumped off the roof.

Chapter 4

Again, it is *Glimpses of the Monastery* that gives the best account of the day after the fire and how the monastery managed to keep going without almost all of its buildings. It even tells us the exact length of time it took to do things. *Glimpses* also provides the story of that earlier fire in 1651.

Records show that Marie-Thérèse returned to the monastery in November of 1685. Her second date of departure isn't recorded, but we know that there were no boarders at the monastery between October 1686 and November 1687. References suggest that she was living with her brother in the spring of 1687. Her return to the monastery to help during the measles epidemic is just a story, but it is something she could have done. The measles epidemic is real, and the nuns did use the washhouse for an infirmary.

Chapter 5

Marie-Thérèse had at least two brothers. Jacques Guyon and Michel Denis Guyon's signatures appear in that order on her marriage document. The priest lists Michel's name first, and "Denis" was Marie-Thérèse's father's name. For these reasons I have assumed that Michel is the elder. Annette, whom I have made Michel's wife, is a completely made-up character. Michel probably was married, but we don't know anything about his wife or about any children they may have had.

The pressure placed on Marie-Thérèse to become a nun is partly historical, but mostly it is a good guess. At sixteen she was a spinster—a strange thing in a country with so few women. There doesn't seem to have been any real family home for her, either. Boarding her at school was expensive. If she became a nun, her brothers would have had to pay a single dowry, but no more boarding fees.

Today, sixteen seems awfully young to be considered an "old maid," but in *Nouvelle France,* it made sense. Because wives were in such short supply, girls and women frequently were imported from Paris just so they could marry *Canadiens.* Girls who were already in Québec were expected to be married and have children as soon as they possibly could—usually when they were thirteen or fourteen years old. The government's desire to increase the population was so strong that young men who weren't married by age sixteen could be fined or receive other penalties.

There was something else happening, too. Women who lived alone generally were not trusted. People felt that women needed protection, of course, but they also thought they needed to be controlled—for their own sake. If a woman didn't get married, the only place this "control" could happen was in a religious order. Although there were women in Québec who actually went into business and made a way for themselves without husbands, they were very rare. All of Québec, not just her brothers, would have expected Marie-Thérèse either to marry or live permanently with the Ursulines.

The globe clock that Marie-Thérèse helps to unpack sounds very modern—like something we'd find today in a novelty shop. Actually, its type was fairly familiar to people in the seventeenth century. Its operation is based on scientific measurements that were known as long ago as the time of the Greeks and Romans. The description of this particular clock is based on a clock built in 1690 and presently kept in a private collection in London, England.

The Language of the Fan was popular throughout the seventeenth and eighteenth century and even part of the nineteenth century. Its exact code varied through the years and from country to country. The version used here includes signals that were common to several fan "languages."

Chapter 6

Now, for the first time, we meet Antoine de Lamothe Cadillac. Exactly how Marie-Thérèse first saw him is not sure. Some people think she could have met him in Port Royal while her father was still living. On the other hand, François Guyon was almost certainly Marie-Thérèse's uncle. Since François and Antoine were business partners in 1687, the year of Marie-Thérèse's marriage to Antoine, I've chosen François as the link. Cadillac's appearance was pretty much as it is described here. When he was in the city, like all wealthy residents of New France, he would have been a stylish dresser. He undoubtedly wore more practical clothing when exploring the wilderness.

Pierre Roy (sometimes spelled Roi) was a real person, but his part in Marie-Thérèse's story is made up. The real Pierre Roy was an explorer and adventurer. He married a woman of the Miami tribe in 1703 and lived with the Miamis who were brought to the Détroit area by Cadillac in 1702 and 1703. So that his Détroit marriage remains possible, I've pretended that it was an earlier marriage that made him Al-soom-se's uncle—but remember that Al-soom-se isn't real anyway!

Chapter 7

Pierre Roy, as I've represented him here, is very much up-to-date on the life of Antoine Laumet de Lamothe Cadillac. Whether the real Pierre Roy knew that much about Antoine or not, the Pierre Roy of the story is telling the truth—as far as we know it today. There is much about Antoine that historians can only suspect. For example, we can only guess why he changed his name. His enemies thought he did so to hide some kind of crime. Modern historians recently have found evidence that Antoine may have had every right to both the Lamothe and Cadillac names and actually may have been the son of one of the younger Cadillacs. Whatever the truth, the fact that being a "de Lamothe Cadillac" helped his army career can't be denied. Antoine himself gave his army rank as lieutenant or captain or just cadet, depending on when he was writing or talking. Once he was in New France, he was given even higher rank in the navy.

After he was in the New World, the degree of support Antoine received from the court of Louis XIV suggests that he came to New France with a direct assignment from the king—more than just a general command to expand the fur trade. Of course we don't know that Antoine was actively seeking a wife at the time he met Marie-Thérèse, but they certainly were married very soon after they met. He must have felt it was the right time to take a bride!

This chapter uses a fictitious tea room as a setting. There, the girls notice gentlemen playing a game of "whist." Whist is much like the card game we now call "bridge."

Chapter 8

It probably would have been unusual for young women to attend a governor's ball under the circumstances described here, but not impossible. Society at the Château St. Louis was like a miniature Versailles (the court of Louis XIV). Because he was expected to entertain in the French manner, Governor Denonville would have kept a small orchestra ready to provide music for his guests. The harpsichord was a favorite instrument in New France, so Anne and other students at the Ursuline school would have been taught to play it. Obviously some students became far better harpsichordists than others did. There is nothing in history to indicate that Anne played particularly well—or even at all—but she could have. And while it may sound strange for nuns to know the latest dances from France, they had to know them! If their pupils were to be taught to be fine ladies, it was necessary for the nuns to be able to dance. Many of the sisters, including Mother Mary of the Angels, joined the Ursulines well into middle age. They remembered the dances they learned as young girls. Then, like the rest of Québec, they waited for the ships crossing the ocean with supplies to bring them news of the latest fashions in dance and dress.

One note of interest: the Jesuit priest mentioned in this chapter was quite an architect. Father Rafaix oversaw the entire reconstruction of the Ursuline monastery after the fire. He is personally responsible for the quick construction of the schoolroom and the emergency work done on the stable chapel. He also supervised construction of many of the permanent buildings that remain there to this day.

Chapter 9

Recorders like the one that Mother St. Esprit plays had been popular for many hundreds of years, even in Marie-Thérèse's time. These were long, carefully shaped, wooden tubes. Melodies were played on them by blowing in the mouthpiece at one end while you covered holes in the side of the tube with your fingers. Recorders came in many sizes. The smaller they were, the higher the notes they played. Mother St. Esprit's recorder was probably a small soprano recorder—one that could play the same tunes that could be played on a violin. Mother St. Esprit probably had to borrow this one, since all the musical instruments belonging to the monastery were destroyed in the fire. I've had her borrow a recorder rather than a violin, since recorders were less valuable and far less easy to break. They probably were much easier to borrow from somebody!

Chapter 10

Romantic tradition and some scholars tell us that Marie-Thérèse first spoke with Antoine Laumet de Lamothe Cadillac at the governor's ball. Once again, this is something we can't know for sure, but we do know what balls were like in those days. We know who was governor. We know how the ladies and gentlemen dressed. In New France, the merchants and storekeepers and their wives would have looked as elegant as if they were lords and ladies at court. There were no dukes and princes in the New World, but all officers in the army and navy were drawn from minor noble classes. The people with the highest positions in society were the people who could make the most money. Many kinds of people were important to the governor, though, and that is why occasionally someone would attend a ball who was not part of "polite society."

Did you notice how the dancers lined up or formed squares for the *contre-danses?* These dances were similar in many ways to the reels and square dances that still are popular today.

Chapter 11

Obviously we don't know much about the first days of Antoine's courtship of Marie-Thérèse. Although François was Antoine's business contact, Michel's name appears on her marriage certificate. From this we assume that it was Michel who was Marie-Thérèse's guardian. There would, of course, have been a dowry—a gift of money or property that accompanied a bride to her new home. And since the Guyon family was a wealthy one (remember that both Marie-Thérèse's father and grandfather had been successful businessmen), the dowry would have been sizeable. It is fair to assume that Cadillac knew this, though we have no way of being sure that it made any difference to him.

There are two important French terms in this chapter. *"Habitant"* is the name given to all French pioneer farmers. *Habitants* were people who lived on, or inhabited, the land. Some were quite wealthy. Others, like Brigitte, were forced to work at odd jobs to bring additional money into the family. The second French word, *portage,* is used to this day to mean the act of carrying a boat or canoe and its heavy contents past unnavigable waters. The *portage* at Niagara Falls (Marie-Thérèse's "great falls") is better than six miles long—a long way to walk on foot, especially if you are carrying well over a hundred (sometimes nearly three hundred) pounds of gear on your back. But that *portage* was part of a well-established trail west—one that everyone (Iroquois, Algonquin, *Canadien*) ultimately agreed was the best and most direct. LaSalle, who explored the lands before Antoine's arrival, built a small fort to protect the route. In 1687, Governor Denonville built a stronger one.

Finally, in this chapter we get a tiny peek at Cadillac's sense of humor. This is something we know quite a bit about. His letters are full of very funny, sarcastic comments about the people with whom he must deal. Many historians talk about Cadillac's "biting wit." If ever a lady did display squeamishness at the terrible things done to people who had been captured by the Iroquois or other tribes, it's a good guess that Cadillac would have laughed first and been comforting later.

Chapter 12

The unusual arrangement surrounding the publication of the banns for Marie-Thérèse and Antoine's marriage is described in her official marriage document. According to it, they were married *"after the betrothal and publication of two banns of marriage, having obtained dispensation of the third from M. de Bernieres, vicar-general of the Lord Bishop of Québec."* The dates of the banns and the date of the wedding are given. The paper says that Marie-Thérèse was "about seventeen years" of age, and Antoine "about twenty-six years" old. As we've already seen, there is some question about how Antoine Laumet came to be known as Antoine de Lamothe Cadillac. In the marriage document itself, Antoine is described as "Antoine de Lamothe, sieur de Cadillac." He signs himself "Lamothe Launay."

"Poor Judith," Antoine and Marie-Thérèse's oldest child, is something of a puzzle. We don't really know for sure that there was anything wrong with her at all, but there is a lot of evidence to suggest she was somehow different from the other children. She never married. In later years she seems to have needed to have someone near her to take care of her all the time. She went to the Ursuline school for two months when she was five years old (August 10–October 3, 1694), but did not return again until August 26, 1701, when she was twelve. For the next four and a half years—except for a three-month period between February 1 and May 4, 1704—she remained at the school along with her younger sister Madeleine. Records show that she left on October 20, 1704. She would have been about fifteen, Madeleine just eight. In 1711 (November 12), Judith, now a middle-aged woman of twenty-two, was back with the Ursulines again. This time she was a pensioner—*en qualité de pensionnaire en chambre,* a lady of quality who lived in a private room near the religious community. Antoine paid 6000 pounds *(livres)* to cover Judith's board "perpetually"—forever—but in 1716 she left the monastery to go with the rest of the family to France. (This sounds like a lot of money—especially in the early 1700s—but for that amount she was assured of a private apartment and special board. 6000 pounds would have been enough to support her fifty years as a student living in the dormitory, but only about twenty-five years as a pensioner.) Once the family was in Castelsarrasin, an unnamed Cadillac daughter, probably Judith, became a pensioner attached to the Carmelite community. Either Judith was extraordinarily devoted to the religious life—but didn't want to become a nun—or something kept her from being part of regular society. Given the number of measles epidemics in *Nouvelle France,* a birth defect is a good guess.

Chapter 13

Marie-Thérèse began married life just about the time that the War of the League of Augsburg broke out. This war was known as "King

William's War" in North America. The situation in *Nouvelle France* in 1690 already was grim, and the war made it worse. Iroquois raids had become severe enough to stop the fur trade altogether, and no one had money. Because the Iroquois were under the protection of English troops, defending French settlements against the Iroquois could be seen as going to war against the English colonists.

In parts of New France, people walled themselves off in forts where they could not raise enough food to eat. Since everyone lived close together, any disease turned into an epidemic. Finally, in one raid near Montreal, the Iroquois captured and tortured ninety settlers. Some of the captives were even eaten by the Iroquois warriors. Because everyone was so afraid, the French troops could do nothing.

Governor Denonville was a good, honest, and respected man, but New France needed a leader who was a general. King Louis sent an experienced explorer, Count Frontenac. Frontenac promptly attacked New York and New England. Some of the Iroquois were chased back to the south, and the Abenaki and Algonquin began to fight harder on the side of the *Canadiens*. When Massachusetts, led by Sir William Phips, attacked Port Royal, it was part of an unsuccessful attempt to change the balance of things to the English. Phips was on his way to Québec at the same time that troops from New York were heading for Montreal. Phips laid siege to Québec, but he was unable to capture the town. He went back home to Massachusetts, his whole venture essentially a failure.

The story of Marie-Thérèse's flight to the forest and her eventual capture by a privateer is true. Not much detail is available, and sometimes it is hard to tell what is history and what is someone's guess about what could have happened. But it is sure that Port Royal suffered damage after—not during—Phips's attack (the soldiers waited to raid the town until after it had surrendered). We know that Marie-Thérèse was ransomed back to her brothers in Québec and stayed there. Marie-Thérèse was not a person to be frightened off just because a place had been attacked once. It is probable that she stayed for a while in Québec because the property in Port Royal was not liveable immediately following Phips's raid.

In Port Royal, Marie-Thérèse's first little house is built of vertical logs *(poteaux en terre)*. Many builders in *Nouvelle France* used the stacked log approach *(pièces sur pièces)*, but since the homes built later at Fort Pontchartrain were of *poteaux en terre* construction, it is likely that this is the method that Antoine preferred.

By the way, American readers will be interested to know that Cadillac's property in Port Royal was right across the river from what is now the state of Maine. He owned many thousands of acres extending on both sides of the present US-Canadian border.

Chapter 14

Marie-Thérèse's long friendship with Anne Picoté de Belestre is made even more interesting by the fact that Anne really did marry Cadillac's second-in-command, Alphonse de Tonty. It was a happy marriage, and we know that they had children who were born at Fort Pontchartrain. For the purposes of this story, I have avoided the question of whether or not the de Tontys had children born before Anne's arrival in Détroit.

Actually, almost all of this chapter is filled with historical facts that we can document (find evidence about). Except for Claudette, Marie-Thérèse's missing helper, and Michel's wife Annette (whose name I've already explained is made up), whenever a specific name is mentioned in chapter 14, it's there because we know it is the correct name for the person involved.

The incredible story of Madeleine de Verchères is still talked about today, especially in the territory south of Montreal where it all happened. Marie-Thérèse tells Madeleine's tale very much the same way that, many years later, Madeleine herself told it to the Marquis de Beauharnois. Then the governor of Canada, the Marquis was something of an historian. He felt that Madeleine's story should be written down and recorded it in his own memoirs.

While there is no direct evidence that little Madeleine de Lamothe Cadillac was named after Madeleine de Verchères, it is a good possibility. Her birth occurred in the spring following the raid on Fort Verchères.

Historical record tells of Antoine's various assignments and awards, and it is especially helpful that Antoine wrote so many letters. Where I've quoted directly from his letters, repeating exactly what Antoine said (except that his words are translated into English) I have put the quotations in italics.

It's true, too, that Marie-Thérèse went to Montreal, where she oversaw purchase and shipment of supplies for her husband at Michilimackinac. She proved to be very good at this duty, which, because timing was so important, was more difficult than ordinary estate management.

Finally, Antoine de Lamothe Cadillac's feud with the Jesuits is as true as it is unfortunate. There was right and wrong on both sides of the argument, just as there is in most arguments. Because of it, some historians today overlook Antoine's achievements and focus on what they see as his exploitation of the natives to whom he gave strong liquor. The impact of the entire issue on history is probably best summed up by Count Frontenac, who described Antoine as *"a man who carries out his duty to the fullest and who is wise, prudent, and perhaps more penetrating than certain people, among whom he must live, would prefer."*

Chapter 15

Any conversation between them, of course, has to be invented, but what Antoine tells Marie-Thérèse about the need for a fort at *le détroit* is exactly what he told anyone who would listen to him. The chronology of this chapter (the order in which things happened) is based on several authorities. Antoine Cadillac's movements between *Nouvelle France* and Paris are well documented. We know when he came back from Fort Michilimackinac and when he went to France. The date of Louis XIV's edict also is a matter of record. However, some sources put Frontenac's death earlier in 1698. I've chosen to use the November time frame described by historian Francis Parkman because it includes a detailed account of Frontenac's conversation with the Récollet priests and probably is based on church records. Finally, it is quite true that Madame Frontenac refused to bury her husband's heart—using almost exactly the words I've attributed to her here!

Chapter 16

Once again, there is a great deal of evidence for nearly everything that is reported in this chapter. Only a few details have been added. The birth of Pierre Denis and Marie Anne, as well as Pierre Denis's death, are matters of record. We don't know what killed Pierre Denis, though crib death (the way it's described here) is always a possibility. One of the reasons people had such large families in the 1600s is that it was the only way to be certain some children would grow to be adults. Marie-Thérèse was extraordinarily lucky not to have lost a child before this time.

When Antoine writes Marie-Thérèse from Paris, the letter, as included here, is made up. However, all the things that he tells her are true, as is Anne's and Marie-Thérèse's description of the ongoing argument between Antoine and the Jesuits. When Antoine talks about what must be done to equip and man the fort at *le détroit,* his conversation is taken from a letter he wrote from Québec on October of 1700 saying much the same thing. (Marie-Thérèse was right about the French preferring to marry their own kind. Pierre Roy was the only man from the first settlement at Fort Pontchartrain to take a native bride.) Antoine's plan to teach French to Abenaki and Ottawa and other braves also didn't work very well. A century later, traders still had to learn the native languages in order to deal successfully. Finally, the memorandum in which de Callières claims the whole venture as his own idea is quoted just as de Callières wrote it— except, of course, that here it is translated into English.

Chapter 17

Antoine's date of departure from Québec and the date that he left Montreal for *le détroit* are listed in contemporary records. It's unsure why Cadillac chose to take one of his younger sons with him and leave the eldest, Joseph, at home. Perhaps Joseph was ill, but since he was one of the healthiest and longest-lived of all the children (he outlived Marie-Thérèse), I've chosen to make the decision involve a question of shared responsibility.

We know when baby Marie Anne died, but as was the case with Pierre Denis, we have no idea why she died. If it was from disease, measles is as good a choice as any. There were many epidemics called "measles" at this time. Almost any disease causing a rash was put in this category—including scarlet fever and rheumatic fever. All of them caused a lot of deaths—especially among small children and the elderly. As for Marie-Thérèse's reaction to Marie Anne's death, that also is just a good guess. A mother who has just lost one baby logically is going to keep a close eye on the next—and be doubly stricken when the second baby dies.

Chapter 18

We do not know how much a part Marie Anne's death played in Marie-Thérèse's determination to go to *le détroit*. But the timing is right for it to have been a matter of some importance—if only that she no longer had to worry about managing a baby in a canoe.

You may have noticed that Al-soom-se has become a kind of happy version of little Agnes Wesk-wes. Since Al-soom-se is a fictitious character, she has chosen a fictitious name for her life in the sisterhood. However it is one that was selected carefully. You will recall that the name "Denise" belonged to a real Abenaki girl. "St. Alexis" is a name frequently used by Ursuline sisters. While Al-soom-se's kinship with Pierre Roy is not real, as we've said, Roy did ultimately marry a native woman. Their descendants may have been among the three ladies surnamed Roy who were lay sisters at the Ursuline monastery in 1875—at the time that the invaluable *Glimpses of the Monastery* was written.

Chapter 19

We know something about how Marie-Thérèse went to Détroit, and recently, with the discovery of the contract between François-Marie Picoté de Belestre and Joseph Trottier Desruisseaux, we know almost exactly when. We can't know all the steps she took in preparation for the trip, but some things are certain.

While Annette, as we've said before, is a fictitious character, her opposition to the trip was shared by the real people whom Marie-Thérèse knew. It was, indeed, an incredibly risky journey for a woman to take. We do have one example of acceptance of—if not support for—Marie-Thérèse's journey. A Jesuit priest, Father Jean Enjalran, wrote to Antoine on August 30, 1701, that he had *"met Mme De Lamothe who is quite set on coming to see you in Détroit."* Enjalran wrote that he wished he could accompany her there, but in the portion of his correspondence available to this author, he does not seem to have criticized her intention to travel. This may reflect the personality of the man himself, or it may come from the way many Jesuits took hardship and danger on the frontier quite for granted. Unfortunately, Enjalran's later dealings with Antoine were not so pleasant. It is Enjalran who most strongly opposed Antoine's desire to encourage whole native populations to resettle near *le détroit*.

François-Marie Picoté de Belestre really was Anne Picoté's younger brother, and he really did contract with the *voyageurs* for passage for Marie-Thérèse, Anne, and their children. I've taken some liberties in making him so much younger than Anne was. He actually was twenty-four at the time of the journey to *le détroit*. He had many other adventures and, in 1752, was living and married to a second wife. At that time, he had a twelve-year-old daughter. He had been in his early sixties at the time he married a young bride and started his second family!

Ursuline records show that Judith and Madeleine went to live at the monastery on August 26, 1701, about a week before the date of the contract with Trottier. It's easy to see that they went to school because their mother could not take them with her to Fort Pontchartrain. They remained at the monastery as regular boarders until February 1, 1704.

The other question in this chapter, why Marie-Thérèse happened to take the southern route to Détroit instead of following Antoine's path, has several answers. First of all, by the fall of 1701, a treaty with the Iroquois finally had been signed. The Iroquois that lived and hunted along the southern route still represented a possible threat to traders and travelers, but at least they had promised to be at peace. Secondly, it couldn't be denied that the trip through Iroquois lands was less demanding in other ways. A single long *portage* at Niagara Falls was far easier to face than the many, many shorter *portages* on the northern route. Finally, the *voyageurs* probably wanted to take the shortest and quickest way possible to *le détroit* to keep from being trapped at Fort Pontchartrain through the winter.

At Fort Pontchartrain, things have progressed rapidly. Antoine's letter to Marie-Thérèse is taken from reports he sent to Count Pontchartrain in Paris and to Callières and de Champigny. In his real letter to Pontchartrain, Antoine asks for more soldiers and says that Father Vaillant is working at cross purposes to him—preventing the Iroquois from trading with him, rather than encouraging them. Count Pontchartrain didn't have much sympathy. He wrote back to Antoine: *"Act in such a manner that the Jesuits become your friends and do not hurt them . . . His Majesty wants the missions around Détroit to be taken care of by the Jesuits."* This can't have made Antoine very happy!

Pierre Roy's role in this chapter is almost entirely fictitious. There is nothing to indicate that he was anywhere around Québec at the time, or indeed had anything to do with Marie-Thérèse's trip up the St.

Lawrence. Just one thing is true: his promise to see Marie-Thérèse at Fort Pontchartrain. Roy was one of Détroit's earliest settlers.

Chapters 20 and 21

The bizarre events of Marie-Thérèse's voyage to Fort Pontchartrain *Ville du Détroit* can be pieced together from the contract signed between François-Marie Picoté de Belestre and Joseph Trottier Desruisseaux and the records from the trial of Joseph Trottier. Trottier was suspected of stealing trade goods from Anne Picoté's canoe and deliberately wintering on Lake Erie in order to trade with local tribes. Since the Québec government wanted all trade to flow through their control (seeing to this was Cadillac's job at Fort Pontchartrain), Trottier's action was doubly illegal.

The contract, dated September 5, 1701, guarantees that the *voyageurs* will be paid a certain price for taking Marie-Thérèse and her party to Fort Pontchartrain—twice that much if they arrive so late that the *voyageurs* must stay at the fort for the winter. Although historians earlier believed that Marie-Thérèse and her party wintered at Fort Frontenac and did not reach *le détroit* until the following spring, the trial records make it clear that the main group made a direct trip all the way to Fort Pontchartrain. If they left Québec in early September, they probably arrived at their destination in mid-October.

It is Father François Vaillant de Gueslis himself who tells us about running into Marie-Thérèse on her way to Fort Pontchartrain. He writes in his memoirs that he worried because she was traveling into danger, but she assured him that she would be safe because she was going to her husband. The words used in this story are the words that Father Vaillant uses in his account of the incident. Since Marie-Thérèse went straight to Détroit and did not spend the winter at Fort Frontenac, such a meeting could have happened during the Niagara Falls *portage,* although conventional wisdom is that their paths crossed much earlier at the fort itself. I have used the later meeting simply because it is possible—and it makes a better story. Father Vaillant talks about the Iroquois kissing the white ladies "rapturously," and Antoine Cadillac wrote of the Iroquois in Détroit kissing "[the ladies'] hands and weeping for joy" that Frenchwomen had come willingly to their country. It is hard to explain this behavior among Iroquois warriors, but I've tried to place the action in a setting that makes sense. Both Antoine and Father Vaillant were trying to make points, and they may have exaggerated to do so.

By the way, Father Vaillant had not been at Détroit long, but it was long enough for Antoine to write a letter to Count Pontchartrain complaining about him!

This part of the story brings out an interesting difference between seventeenth- and eighteenth-century standards of cleanliness and those

185

we know today. Québec, as we have said, was very advanced in its keeping of sewage in a drain in the middle of the streets, away from the houses. Housewives worked to keep their homes tidy and attractive. Keeping personal clothing clean and neat was always important, and Marie-Thérèse certainly knew that clean hands and faces were a good idea. But this was a time when bathing carried with it the risk of chill and disease; too much of it wasn't considered healthy. Marie-Thérèse and Anne didn't care much for the way the Iroquois smelled. (And no wonder! Bear grease—rendered bear fat—when used as a skin cream, was allowed to become rancid, and often was mixed with skunk oil.) But when Marie-Thérèse and Anne have to make themselves smell a little better for their arrival at Fort Pontchartrain (remember, they've been traveling for weeks and haven't bathed in all that time) they count on perfume—not washing—to make themselves presentable.

There was great celebration at Fort Pontchartrain after Marie-Thérèse's arrival. Everyone feasted on deer and bear and *sagamité,* a kind of stew. Many tribes were represented, from the Ottawa to the north to the Potawatomi and Miami who lived south and west of *le détroit.* All the warriors were curious to see Cadillac's woman. Trade goods came with the arriving canoes, and gifts of beads and other trade stuffs were made to all who were there. Antoine knew that the Iroquois in particular loved a fine show. That is one of the reasons he dressed up to meet Marie-Thérèse, and why she knew to dress in her finest before she approached the fort.

Marie-Thérèse's life story has only begun with her arrival in Détroit. However, once she arrived at Fort Pontchartrain, she was ready to rest for a while. So is this book.

After the Story

Marie-Thérèse and Antoine lived in Détroit for almost ten years. Then, in 1711, Antoine was made governor of Louisiana. He led an attempt to colonize what is now Baton Rouge. Mosquitoes and disease and hostile natives made settling there almost impossible, but Marie-Thérèse and Antoine kept trying. In 1716, they made separate trips to France seeking more colonists and royal support for their venture, but by then King Louis XIV was dead. His grandson, King Louis XV, was just a little boy. The young king's advisors were busy paying the royal debts and had no interest in spending money on the settling of New France. Antoine wanted to explore further into what is now Illinois, but his enemies picked this time to work even harder against him. For Marie-Thérèse and Antoine, there were to be no more trips to the New World.

Did you want to know if it was true that Marie-Thérèse freed her husband and her brother-in-law from the famous Bastille prison? Oh, yes indeed. How they got there and how she rescued them is a sad but exciting part of their early years back home in France.

After the Bastille episode, a little more time went by and Antoine was made governor of Castelsarrasin. There the family lived comfortably, and Antoine eventually was awarded the Cross of St. Louis for his many services to the old king. Antoine continued as governor of Castelsarrasin until his death in 1730. Marie-Thérèse lived for sixteen more years. She was seventy-five years old when she died. In 1746, that was considered a respectable old age.

In the years that they were married, Antoine and Marie-Thérèse had a total of thirteen children. Five of the children died when they were very small. Only Joseph, the eldest son, and François and little Marie-Thérèse (both of whom were born at Fort Pontchartrain) outlived their parents. Today there are no living direct descendants of Antoine and Marie-Thérèse Cadillac, but the stories of their adventures belong to us all.

A Note about the Indian Population of New France

Most of the native peoples mentioned in the early part of *First Lady* are Abenaki. This has been done more in the interest of providing a consistent naming convention than of historical accuracy. The native peoples of eastern North America included many nations and subdivisions of nations. In fact, Antoine Laumet de Lamothe Cadillac's vision of the fur trade depended in large part on the gathering of many peoples from many tribes. The Ursuline monastery in Québec served not only the Abenaki, but also Hurons, Algonquins, and even Iroquois—though Algonquins and Hurons tended to be dominant among monastery pupils. (I have no real justification for making Al-soom-se Abenaki, except that she seemed to want to be so.) Readers will note that I have tried to avoid use of the currently controversial term "Indian" or "American Indian," but I am equally determined not to use the euphemism "Native American." "America" and "American" are words dependent on the existence of an Italian mapmaker named Amerigo Vespucci—called "Americus Vespucius" by scholars. I find little to connect him with the history of New France.

THE CHILDREN OF
ANTOINE AND MARIE-THÉRÈSE CADILLAC

Antoine and Marie-Thérèse had many children—thirteen in all. Such large families were not as unusual three hundred years ago as they are today. So many children died from disease that parents knew they would need to have two or three children to be sure that just one might live to grow up. Actually, there may have been more than thirteen Cadillac children. These are the ones of whom we know.

Name	Birth Date	Comment	Last Mentioned
Judith	1689	Probably born in Port Royal or Québec. Never married	Possibly is daughter who lived with Carmelite nuns in Castelsarrasin after 1716
Joseph	1690	Probably born in Port Royal or Québec. Married Marguerite de Gregoire	Daughter's baptism listed in Church of the Savior (Castelsarrasin) records in 1733
Antoine	April 26, 1692	Probably born in Québec. Came to Détroit with his father in 1701	Entered military service
Madeleine	circa 1693	Born in Port Royal or Mt. Desert.	Left Ursuline school in 1716 after her third stay there, probably to go with family to France. Her board was paid by a "M. Morin"
Jacques	March 16, 1695	Born in Québec. Came to Détroit with Marie-Thérèse	No further information

188

Antoine and Marie Thérèse's Children

Name	Birth Date	Comment	Last Mentioned
Pierre Denis	June 13, 1699	Born in Québec. Named for Marie-Thérèse's father and brother	Died July 4, 1700 (age 1 year)
Marie Anne	June 7, 1700	Born in Québec	Died June 9, 1701 (age 1 year)
"Child"	Fall 1702	Born in Détroit, mentioned in a letter from Cadillac	Died a few days or weeks after birth (age 0 to 2 months)
Marie-Thérèse	*February 2, 1704	Born in Détroit. Married François Hercule de Pouzargues in Castelsarrasin, February 16, 1729. No children	Died February 1, 1753 (age 49 years)
Jean Antoine	*January 19, 1707	Born in Détroit	Died April 9, 1709 (age 2 years)
Marie Agathe	December 28, 1707	Born in Détroit and baptized the next day	No further mention. May have died in Détroit or Louisiana
François	March 27, 1709	Born in Détroit. Some records say he may have been born in 1703. Married Angelique Furgole. No children	Living in Castelsarrasin during Marie-Thérèse's old age
René Louis	March 17, 1710	Born in Détroit and baptized the next day	Died and was buried in Québec October 7, 1714 (age 4 years)

*Date of baptism.

BIBLIOGRAPHY

Archives of the Ursulines of Québec, 1639–present. (Research performed by Marie Marchand, o.s.u., and Louise Godin, o.s.u., April–June 2000, Quebec).

Berg, Harriet. Interview by author, March 20, 2000, Detroit. Transcript. Author's collection, Rochester.

Berg, Harriet, and Donna Raphael. *Mme. Cadillac Dance Theatre.* Detroit: Owl Printing, ca. 1992.

Braun & Schneider, ed. *Historic Costume in Pictures* (orig. title: *Costumes of All Nations.* London: H. Grevel and Co., 1907). Dover Pictorial Archive Series. Reprint, New York: Dover Publications, Inc., 1975.

Brown, Henry D., Henri Négrié, Frank R. Place, René Toujas, Leonard N. Simons, Solan Weeks, et al. *Cadillac and the Founding of Detroit.* Detroit: Wayne State University Press, 1976.

Burton, Clarence M. "A Sketch of the Life of Antoine de La Mothe Cadillac, Founder of Detroit, Part 7," *Michigan's Habitant Heritage* 21, no. 1 (January 2000): 6–8.

Campeau, Anita R., and Gail F. Moreau. "Translation of and Commentary on Trial of Joseph Trottier Desruisseaux," *Michigan's Habitant Heritage* 21, no. 1 (January 2000): 10–17.

Campeau, Anita R., and Gail F. Moreau. "Translation of Contract to Bring Madame Cadillac and Madame Tonty to Detroit," *Michigan's Habitant Heritage* 21, no. 1 (January 2000): 9–10.

Dancetime! 500 Years of Social Dance. Vol. 1, *15th–16th Centuries.* 45 min. Produced by Dance through Time with artistic direction by Carol Teton. Dance through Time, 1999. Videocassette.

Glimpses of the Monastery: A Brief Sketch of the History of the Ursulines of Quebec During Two Hundred Years, by a Member of the Community. Part 2, *From 1672 to 1739.* Québec: C. Darveau, 1875.

Kalman, Bobbie. *18th Century Clothing.* Historic Communities. Ontario: Crabtree Publishing Company, 1993.

Kent, Timothy. Interview by author, February 3, 2001, Ossineke, MI. Transcript. Author's collection, Rochester.

Laut, Agnes C. Cadillac, *Knight Errant of the Wilderness, Founder of Detroit, Governor of Louisiana from the Great Lakes to the Gulf.* Indianapolis: Bobbs-Merrill Company, 1931.

Lower, Arthur R. M. *Canadians in the Making: A Social History of Canada.* Westport: Greenwood Publishing Group, 1981.

Mahoney, Mother Denis, o.s.u. *Marie of the Incarnation: Mystic and Missionary.* Garden City: Doubleday and Company, 1964.

Parkman, Francis. *France and England in North America,* vols. 1 and 2. New York: Literary Classics of the United States, Inc., 1983.

Raffety and Walwyn. *Antique Clocks and Barometers.* http://www.raffetyantiqueclocks.com; Internet; accessed May 8, 2000.

Souvenir of the Unveiling of the Tablet Presented by the Women's Bi-Centenary Committee in Memory of Madame de la Mothe Cadillac. Detroit: Detroit Museum of Art, 1903.

Trudel, Marcel. *Introduction to New France.* Toronto: Holt, Rinehart and Winston of Canada. Reprint, Pawtucket, RI: Quintin Publications, 1997.

Trudel, Marcel. *Les écolières des Ursulines de Québec: 1639–1686, Amérindiennes et Canadiennes.* Montréal: Université du Québec, 1999.

Woodford, Frank B., and Arthur M. Woodford. *All Our Yesterdays: A Brief History of Detroit.* Detroit: Wayne State University Press, 1969.

Wussman, Jesse. *A Brief History of Clocks: From Thales to Ptolemy.* http://www.perseus.tufts.edu/GreekScience/Students/Jesse/CLOCK1A.html; Internet; accessed May 8, 2000.

First
Lady of Detroit